FAMILY HOME EVENING

ADVENTURES

FAMILY HOME EVENING

ADVENTURES

REBECCA IRVINE

HORIZON PUBLISHERS,
SPRINGVILLE, UT

ISBN 13: 978-0-88290-971-4

Published by Horizon Publishers, an imprint of Cedar Fort, Inc., 2373 W. 700 S., Springville, UT 84663
Distributed by Cedar Fort, Inc. www.cedarfort.com

Cover design by Angela D. Olsen
Cover design © 2009 by Lyle Mortimer
Edited and typeset by Melissa J. Caldwell

Printed in the United States of America

10 9 8 7 6 5 4 3 2 1

Printed on acid-free paper

To Patrick, Katie, and Emily,
the three best children I could have ever received.
You are the greatest blessings in my life.

Contents

INTRODUCTION—IX

JANUARY—1
Reverence

FEBRUARY—8
Love at Home

MARCH—16
Heavenly Treasure

APRIL—23
The Atonement

MAY—27
Mother's Day

JUNE—32
Father's Day

CONTENTS

JULY — 38
Freedom and Liberty

AUGUST — 43
Preparing for Baptism

SEPTEMBER — 49
Faith BINGO

OCTOBER — 59
Law of the Harvest

NOVEMBER — 66
Feast Upon the Word

DECEMBER — 74
Journey to Bethlehem

ABOUT THE AUTHOR — 83

Introduction

Family Home Evening Adventures can help your family learn to love and enjoy the scriptures together. Each monthly theme uses fun seasonal ideas to promote an appreciation of scripture study, teach basic gospel principles, and provide wholesome family activities. Families read a set of themed scriptures and then work together to solve puzzles, answer questions, and build budding testimonies. The hands-on activities and visuals aids help children remember the lessons learned from the scriptures during family home evening.

By using Family Home Evening Adventures, you can involve younger children and help them look forward to family home evenings and other scripture study opportunities. Start by copying and cutting out the visual aids for each lesson. Use markers, colored pencils, or crayons, and scissors, glue, and other simple supplies to help prepare theme pieces as instructed. During the lesson, present the visual aids on a bulletin board, poster board, wall, or kitchen cupboard. Displayed all month long, the visual aids will serve as a reminder of the important principles that were taught during family night.

In addition to the visual aids included in Family Home Evening Adventures, each lesson offers the following resources to help enhance your family home evening experiences:

1. A game or activity
2. Suggested song choices
3. A story reference from the Friend
4. A thought-provoking quote
5. A fun treat idea

PLANNING FOR SUCCESS

Family Home Evening Adventures provides one lesson plan for each month of the year. Since family home evenings provide parents with some of their best opportunities for teaching children to love the scriptures, planning lessons ahead of time can help ensure the highest quality teaching time. Use the following step-by-step strategy to plan a year's worth of lesson topics in advance.

1. Using the following planning sheet, write down all the dates of the Mondays in the upcoming year (or whatever day of the week your family holds FHE).

2. Check these dates and make a note next to each one that is a family member's birthday, a major holiday, or a time when your family will be out of town. You will likely not be having a standard lesson on those weeks.

3. Plan a lesson topic for each week of the month. For example, your topics may look something like this:

Week 1—Lesson from the *Friend* magazine

Week 2—Lesson from FHE manual

Week 3—Lesson from *FHE Adventures*

Week 4—Lesson from most recent conference issue of the *Ensign*

Week 5—Family activity

In addition to these topic selections, your family might enjoy lessons based on scripture parables, seminary scripture mastery scriptures, chapters from the Relief Society/Priesthood manual (or past manuals), the Gospel Essentials manual, the *For the Strength of Youth* pamphlet, or other help books available at LDS bookstores.

On the planning sheet, write your preferred topics next to each appropriate week. If you are using a manual of some sort, be sure to include a chapter number so as to eliminate duplication in case someone forgets what was taught in previous months.

4. Decide a set rotation of who will be assigned the lessons. Make sure each family member has the opportunity to teach at some point during the year, but also take into consideration the age-appropriateness of the lesson topics and resources previously selected. Write the names down on the planning sheet. This is your completed plan!

5. Post your schedule in a safe place, so you can refer to it throughout the year.

Family Home Evening Planning Sheet

Date		Teacher	Lesson	Date		Teacher	Lesson
January				July			
	Week 1				Week 1		
	Week 2				Week 2		
	Week 3				Week 3		
	Week 4				Week 4		
	(Week 5)				(Week 5)		
February				August			
	Week 1				Week 1		
	Week 2				Week 2		
	Week 3				Week 3		
	Week 4				Week 4		
					(Week 5)		
March				September			
	Week 1				Week 1		
	Week 2				Week 2		
	Week 3				Week 3		
	Week 4				Week 4		
	(Week 5)				(Week 5)		
April				October			
	Week 1				Week 1		
	Week 2				Week 2		
	Week 3				Week 3		
	Week 4				Week 4		
	(Week 5)				(Week 5)		
May				November			
	Week 1				Week 1		
	Week 2				Week 2		
	Week 3				Week 3		
	Week 4				Week 4		
	(Week 5)				(Week 5)		
June				December			
	Week 1				Week 1		
	Week 2				Week 2		
	Week 3				Week 3		
	Week 4				Week 4		
	(Week 5)				(Week 5)		

ADDITIONAL HELPFUL HINTS AND SUGGESTIONS

1. For most of the visual aids in *Family Home Evening Adventures,* the actual scripture verses are included on the backs of the theme pieces. This eliminates the time needed to look up the verses in the standard works and streamlines the lesson. However, for older children who may need experience looking up scriptures and finding verses, parents may prefer to put only the references on the backs of the visual aids.

2. Repetition is one of the keys to learning. After beginning the lesson, ask children the same question about each of the scriptures. For example, for the month of February and the lesson about Love at Home, you may ask, "What does this scripture teach us that can help us to have more love at home?" Asking the same question helps children to anticipate what answers to listen for in the scripture verses and teaches them to pay closer attention.

3. Use a bulletin board or other flat surface in a convenient area of the home to present the lesson, and have children take turns placing the visual aid pieces. Kids love to put the theme pieces up and enjoy seeing the progress made as more are added. This hands-on interaction helps involve all family members in the learning process.

4. Take time to define new words in the scriptures. Often the scriptural verses read very differently than the modern language more commonly used. Help clarify what the scriptures say by giving familiar examples and common definitions of terms or phrases.

5. Although it can be difficult to get everyone together at the same time and in a cooperative mood, parents should be conscious of their own attitudes and do everything possible to make home evening time positive and happy, so the Spirit can be present.

JANUARY

REVERENCE

Objective: To help family members understand the importance of being reverent and how to act in a reverent manner, especially during Church meetings.

Directions: Copy the snowflake page three times and the chapel picture one time onto a heavy-weight paper. Cut out the snowflakes in a circular shape. Copy and cut out the reverence scriptures and then glue them to the back of the snowflakes. Laminate the snowflakes and chapel picture for more durability if desired. To make a reverence mobile, use a hole punch to make one hole in the top of each snowflake and in the top corners of the chapel picture. Hang the chapel picture from a hanger. Have eighteen varied lengths of string or yarn ready for use during the lesson to attach the snowflakes to the mobile.

Lesson: Explain to family members that the definition of reverence is "a feeling or attitude of deep respect tinged with awe." Read the snowflake scriptures and discuss each briefly; after each is read, hang the snowflake from the hanger to form a mobile. Teach family members that in the scriptures, one synonym for reverence is to "fear the Lord." This does not mean to be afraid, but means to show respect.

Have family members brainstorm ideas of how reverence is shown outwardly; these may include some of the following:

* Bowing head, folding arms, and closing eyes during prayers.
* Keeping voices to a whisper.
* Refraining from leaving the chapel during sacrament meeting.
* Thinking of the Savior during the sacrament.
* Joining the congregation in singing hymns.
* Keeping hands and feet still or quiet during meetings.
* Showing respect for leaders, at home, church, school, or in the community.

Hang the reverence mobile in your home for the month as a visual reminder.

Activity: Practice reverent behaviors during family home evening by playing the game "Night at the Museum." To play, choose one family member to be the museum night watchman. All other family members are statues. The night watchman turns the lights off. In the dark the statues strike a pose showing a reverent behavior. Using a flashlight, the night watchman shines light on one statue at a time and tries to guess the behavior shown. Have family members take turns being the night watchman.

SCRIPTURES

Exodus 3:4–5	Psalm 119:15	3 Nephi 11:12
Exodus 20:12	Proverbs 3:9	3 Nephi 11:17
Leviticus 19:30	Isaiah 17:7	3 Nephi 14:12
Deuteronomy 10:12	Hebrews 12:9	Moroni 6:9
1 Samuel 12:24	2 Nephi 25:29	D&C 84:54–56
Psalms 89:7	Alma 34:38	D&C 109:21

ADDITIONAL RESOURCES:

Music: "Reverently, Quietly" (*Children's Songbook*, 26); "The Chapel Doors" (*Children's Songbook*, 156); "Our Savior's Love" (*Hymns*, no. 113).

Story: Lisa Ray Turner, "Alisa's Plan," *Friend*, Sep. 1996, 30.

Quote: "To truly reverence the Creator, we must appreciate His creations. We need to take time to observe the marvels of nature. We can easily become surrounded by brick buildings and asphalt surfaces that shelter us from the real life around us. Share with your family the miracle of buds changing to fragrant blossoms. Take time to sit on a hillside and feel the tranquility of the evening when the sun casts its last golden glow over the horizon. Take time to smell the roses," (M. Russell Ballard, "Take Time," *Friend*, Nov. 1992, inside front cover).

Suggested Treat: Cupcakes frosted with white frosting and dusted with coconut to resemble snowballs.

Furthermore we have had fathers of our flesh which corrected us, and we gave them reverence: shall we not much rather be in subjection unto the Father of spirits.
(Hebrews 12:9)

Ye shall keep my sabbaths, and reverence my sanctuary: I am the Lord.
(Leviticus 19:30)

I will meditate in thy precepts, and have respect unto thy ways.
(Psalm 119:15)

At that day shall a man look to his Maker, and his eyes shall have respect to the Holy One of Israel.
(Isaiah 17:7)

For in six days the Lord made heaven and earth, the sea, and all that in them is, and rested the seventh day: wherefore the Lord blessed the sabbath day, and hallowed it.
(Exodus 20:11)

Honour the Lord with thy substance, and with the firstfruits of all thine increase.
(Proverbs 3:9)

And now, Israel, what doth the Lord thy God require of thee, but to fear the Lord thy God, to walk in all his ways, and to love him, and to serve the Lord thy God with all thy heart and with all thy soul.
(Deuteronomy 10:12)

Only fear the Lord, and serve him in truth with all your heart: for consider how great things he hath done for you.
(1 Samuel 12:24)

Therefore, all things whatsoever ye would that men should do to you, do ye even so to them; for this is the law and the prophets.
(3 Nephi 14:12)

And it came to pass that when Jesus had spoken these words the whole multitude fell to the earth; for they remembered that it had been prophesied among them that Christ should show himself unto them after his ascension into heaven.
(3 Nephi 11:12)

And your minds in times past have been darkened because of un-belief, and because you have treated lightly the things you have received— Which vanity and unbelief have brought the whole church under condemnation. And this condemna-tion resteth upon the children of Zion, even all.
(D&C 84:54–56)

And when the Lord saw that he turned aside to see, God called unto him out of the midst of the bush, and said, Moses, Moses. And he said, Here am I. And he said, Draw not nigh hither: put off thy shoes from off thy feet, for the place whereon thou standest is holy ground.
(Exodus 3:4–5)

God is greatly to be feared in the assembly of the saints, and to be had in reverence of all them that are about him.
(Psalm 89:7)

And when thy people transgress, any of them, they may speedily repent and return unto thee, and find favor in thy sight, and be restored to the blessings which thou hast ordained to be poured out upon those who shall reverence thee in thy house.
(D&C 109:21)

And now behold, I say unto you that the right way is to believe in Christ, and deny him not; and Christ is the Holy One of Israel; wherefore ye must bow down before him, and worship him with all your might, mind, and strength, and your whole soul; and if ye do this ye shall in nowise be cast out.
(2 Nephi 25:29)

That ye contend no more against the Holy Ghost, but that ye receive it, and take upon you the name of Christ; that ye humble yourselves even to the dust, and worship God, in whatsoever place ye may be in, in spirit and in truth; and that ye live in thanksgiving daily, for the many mercies and blessings which he doth bestow upon you.
(Alma 34:38)

Hosanna! Blessed be the name of the Most High God! And they did fall down at the feet of Jesus, and did worship him.
(3 Nephi 11:17)

And their meetings were conducted by the church after the manner of the workings of the Spirit, and by the power of the Holy Ghost; for as the power of the Holy Ghost led them whether to preach, or to exhort, or to pray, or to supplicate, or to sing, even so it was done.
(Moroni 6:9)

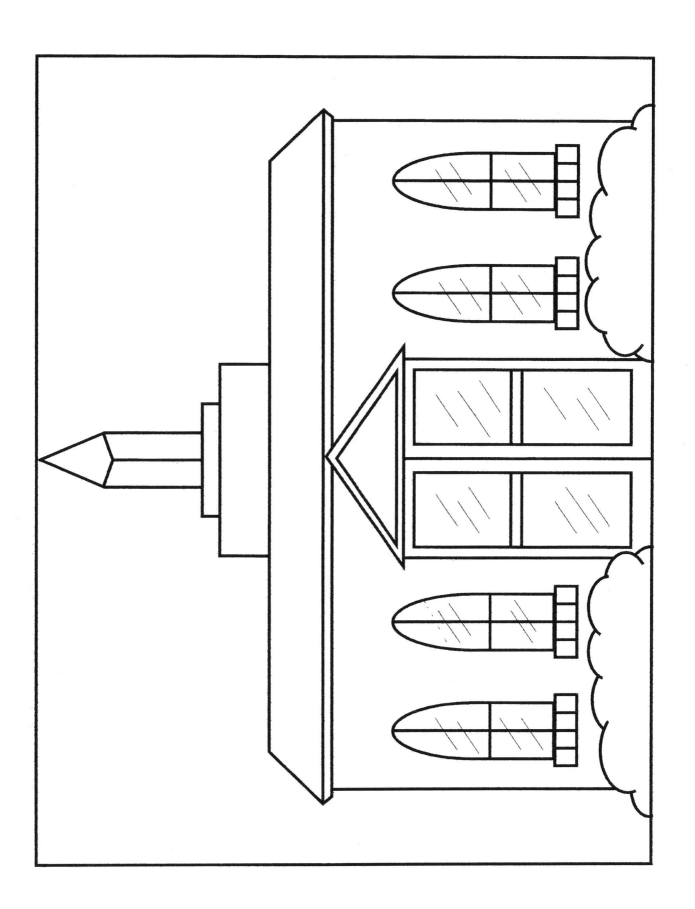

FEBRUARY

LOVE AT HOME

Objective: To help teach family members the importance of showing love for one another in the home.

Directions: Copy each of the six house pages onto cardstock. Cut out and glue the light gray version of the house together. Cut out, glue together, and color the black version of the house. Using an exacto knife, cut along the dotted lines where the panels will open to show the scripture verses. Glue the black version of the house on top of the gray version, being careful not to get glue behind any of the openings.

Lesson: Begin your family home evening lesson by opening panel one. Read the scripture and discuss its importance. Using what the scriptures teach, write down ways that will help families to have greater love at home. Continue reading each scripture in order, much like an advent calendar. After all the scriptures are read, encourage family members to choose one of the behaviors or teachings they could work on for the month. Have each member write a goal on a paper heart. Display the hearts and the scripture house in your home for the month as a visual reminder.

Activity: Randomly assign each family member the name of someone else in the family. Sit in a circle and have one person begin describing their family member using only loving and positive words, but without giving the person's name. Other family members must guess who is being described. Take turns until every name has been guessed.

SCRIPTURES

Genesis 18:19	Ephesians 6:4	Mosiah 4:14–15
Proverbs 13:24	Colossians 3:19–20	Moroni 7:45
Ecclesiastes 9:9	1 Timothy 5:1–2	Moroni 8:17
Malachi 4:5–6	Titus 2:4	D&C 88:123
Matthew 18:10	1 John 2:10	D&C 93:40
Mark 10:7–9	1 Nephi 1:1	D&C 121:41–43
John 13:34	1 Nephi 8:37	D&C 131:2
John 14:15	2 Nephi 2:25	Moses 6:58
1 Corinthians 11:11	2 Nephi 25:26	
Ephesians 5:25	Mosiah 1:2	

ADDITIONAL RESOURCES:

Music: "Families Can Be Together Forever" (*Children's Songbook,* 188); "Love is Spoken Here" (*Children's Songbook,* 190); "Love at Home" (*Hymns,* no. 294).

Story: Janice Graham, "The Butler Did It," *Friend,* May 1999, 16

Quote: "There is no substitute for the home. Its foundation is as ancient as the world, and its mission has been ordained of God from the earliest times. . . . There can be no genuine happiness separate and apart from the home, and every effort made to sanctify and preserve its influence is uplifting to those who toil and sacrifice for its establishment. There is no happiness without service, and there is no greater service than that which converts the home into a divine institution, and which promotes and preserves family life," (Joseph F. Smith as quoted by Rex D. Pinegar, " 'Home First,' " *Ensign,* May 1990, 9).

Suggested Treat: Sugar cookies cut out in heart and house shapes.

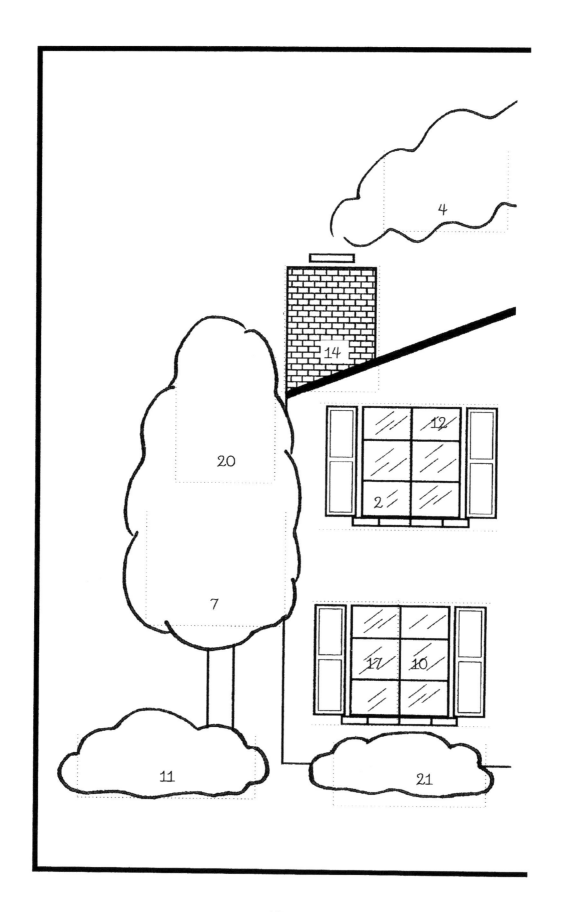

ve at Home ♥

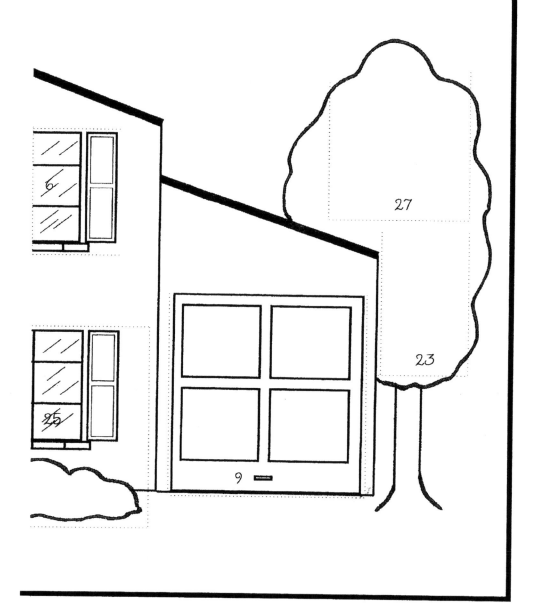

Husbands, love your wives, even as Christ also loved the church and gave himself for it. (Ephesians 5:25)

He that spareth his rod hateth his son: but he that loveth him chasteneth him betimes. (Proverbs 13:24)

Live joyfully with the wife whom thou lovest all the days of the life of thy vanity, which he hath given thee under the sun, all the days of thy vanity. (Ecclesiastes 9:9)

If ye love me, keep my commandments. (John 14:15)

Teach the young women to be sober, to love their husbands, to love their children. (Titus 2:4)

Take heed that ye despise not one of these little ones; for I say unto you, That in heaven their angels do always behold the face of my Father which is in heaven. (Matthew 18:10)

Adam fell that men might be; and men are, that they might have joy. (2 Nephi 2:25)

I have commanded you to bring up your children in light and truth. (D&C 93:40)

A new commandment I give unto you, That ye love one another; as I have loved you, that ye also love one another. (John 13:34)

Therefore, I give unto you a commandment, to teach these things freely unto your children. (Moses 6:58)

And in order to obtain the highest (degree of glory), a man must enter into this order of the priesthood [meaning the new and everlasting covenant of marriage]. (D&C 131:2)

And we talk of Christ, we rejoice in Christ, we preach of Christ, we prophesy of Christ, and we write according to our prophecies, that our children may know to what source they may look for a remission of their sins. (2 Nephi 25:26)

For I know him, that he will command his children and his household after him, and they shall keep the way of the Lord, to do justice and judgment. (Genesis 18:19)

He that loveth his brother abideth in the light, and there is none occasion of stumbling in him. (1 John 2:10)

Nevertheless neither is the man without the woman, neither the woman without the man, in the Lord. (1 Corinthians 11:11)

And charity suffereth long, and is kind, and envieth not, and is not puffed up, seeketh not her own, is not easily provoked, thinketh no evil, and rejoiceth not in iniquity but rejoiceth in the truth, beareth all things, believeth all things, hopeth all things, endureth all things. (Moroni 7:45)

And, ye fathers, provoke not your children to wrath: but bring them up in the nurture and admonition of the Lord. (Ephesians 6:4)

Behold, I will send you Elijah the prophet before the coming of the great and dreadful day of the Lord: And he shall turn the heart of the fathers to the children, and the heart of children to their fathers, lest I come and smite the earth with a curse. (Malachi 4:5–6)

And I am filled with charity, which is everlasting love; wherefore, all children are alike unto me; wherefore, I love little children with a perfect love; and they are all partakers of salvation. (Moroni 8:17)

See that ye love one anther; cease to be covetous; learn to impart one to another as the gospel requires. (D&C 88:123)

For this cause shall a man leave his father and mother, and cleave to his wife; And they twain shall be one flesh: so then they are no more twain, but one flesh. What therefore God hath joined together, let not man put asunder. (Mark 10:7–9)

14

And he caused that they should be taught in all the language of his fathers, that thereby they might become men of understanding; and that they might know concerning the prophecies which had been spoken by the mouths of their fathers, which were delivered by the hand of the Lord.
(Mosiah 1:2)

No power or influence can or ought to be maintained by virtue of the priesthood, only by persuasion, by longsuffering, by gentlenss and meekness, and by love unfeigned; By kindness, and pure knowledge, which shall greatly inlarge the soul without hypocrisy, and without guile—Reproving betimes with sharpness, when moved upon by the Holy Ghost; and then showing forth afterwards an increase of love toward him whom thou hast reproved, lest he esteem thee to be his enemy. (D&C 121:41–43)

Husbands, love your wives. . . . Children, obey your parents in all things; for this is well pleasing unto the Lord.
(Colossians 3:19–20)

And [Lehi] did exhort them then with all the feeling of a tender parent, that they would hearken to his words, that perhaps the Lord would be merciful to them, and not cast them off; yea, my father did preach unto them.
(1 Nephi 8:37)

Rebuke not an elder, but intreat him as a father and the younger men as brethren; The elder women as mothers; the younger as sisters, with all purity.
(1 Timothy 5:1–2)

I, Nephi, having been born of goodly parents, therefore I was taught somewhat in all the learning of my father; and having seen many afflictions in the course of my days, nevertheless, having been highly favored of the Lord in all my days; yea, having had a great knowledge of the goodness and the mysteries of God, therefore I make a record of my proceedings in my days.
(1 Nephi 1:1)

And ye will not suffer your children that they go hungry, or naked; neither will ye suffer that they transgress the laws of God, and fight and quarrel one with another. . . . But ye will teach them to walk in the ways of truth and soberness; ye will teach them to love one another; and to serve one another.
(Mosiah 4:14–15)

2010

MARCH
HEAVENLY TREASURE

Object: To help family members understand those things that have eternal value as compared to temporal or earthly objects.

Directions: Copy the Celestial Cents page three times onto gold or yellow cardstock; copy the pot of gold, rainbow, and the scripture circles once each on plain white paper. Cut out the Celestial Cents and the scriptures and then glue the scriptures to the back of the Celestial Cents. Color and cut out the rainbow. Cut out the pot of gold. Laminate the Celestial Cents, pot, and rainbow for durability, if desired. Attach the pot of gold to the front of a sturdy paper bag or gift bag (one that is approximately six to eight inches wide works best). Attach the rainbow to the interior on the backside of the bag. Place the Celestial Cents in the bag.

Lesson: Remind family members of the legend that great treasure can be found at the end of the rainbow. Explain that temporal or earthly treasures are very different from what Heavenly Father feels is most valuable. Show family members the special pot of gold. Explain that inside the bag are Celestial Cents, which give clues to what Father in Heaven treasures. Pull out one Celestial Cent from the bag, read the scripture, and determine with family members what item of value is being discussed. Repeat until all the Celestial Cent scriptures have been read.

Activity: Assign a monetary value to each of the Celestial Cents. Set a family goal for completing daily scripture study during the month. After each completed study session, reward the family with a Celestial Cent. At the end of the month add up the value earned and then spend it on a family outing for ice cream or another activity. Discuss with family members how this delayed reward is much like "laying up treasures in heaven" through obedience to the commandments.

SCRIPTURES

Exodus 19:5	John 2:14–15	D&C 14:7
Deuteronomy 28:12	Colossians 3:16	D&C 15:6
Proverbs 15:6	Joseph Smith—Matthew 1:37	D&C 18:10
Isaiah 33:5–6	1 Nephi 5:21	D&C 19:38
Matthew 10:29–31	Alma 9:21–23	D&C 43:34
Mark 12:42–44	D&C 6:3	D&C 89:18–19

ADDITIONAL RESOURCES:

Music: "My Heavenly Father Loves Me" (*Children's Songbook*, 228); "Search, Ponder, and Pray" (*Children's Songbook*, 109); "Dearest Children" (*Hymns*, no. 96)

Story: Helen Hughes Vick, "The Very Best Gift," *Friend*, May 1994, 2

Quote: "It is obvious that treasures found in the world cannot give that which people hope for. Many people have to live an entire lifetime to find out in the end that with all the treasures and riches of the world they have gathered, they have not found the real treasure. They remain empty, unhappy, dissatisfied, and plagued with growing fears. The miracle of the only real treasure is that it constantly produces blessings and the overcoming of fears. I am speaking about the treasure of having found Christ," (F. Enzio Busche, "The Only Real Treasure," *New Era*, Dec. 1979, 4).

Suggested Treat: Chocolate coins

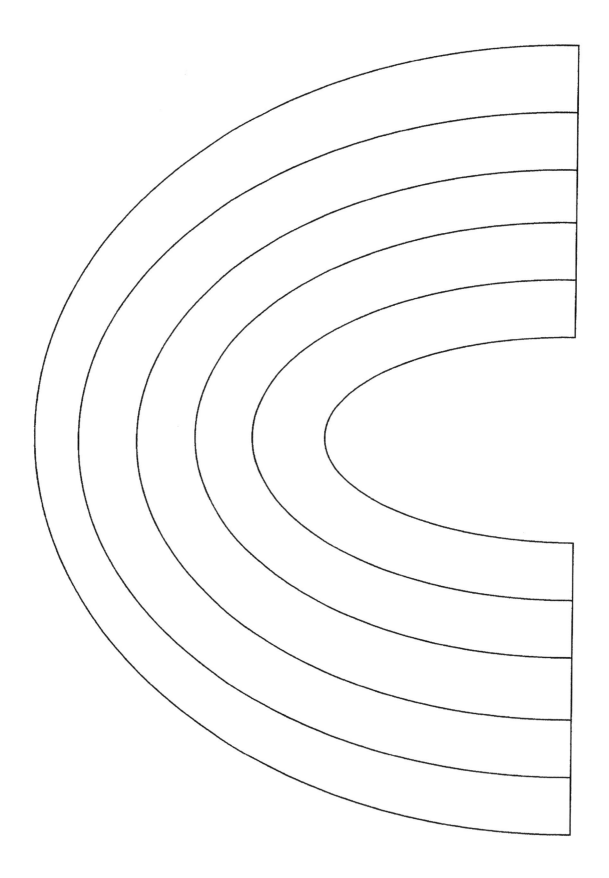

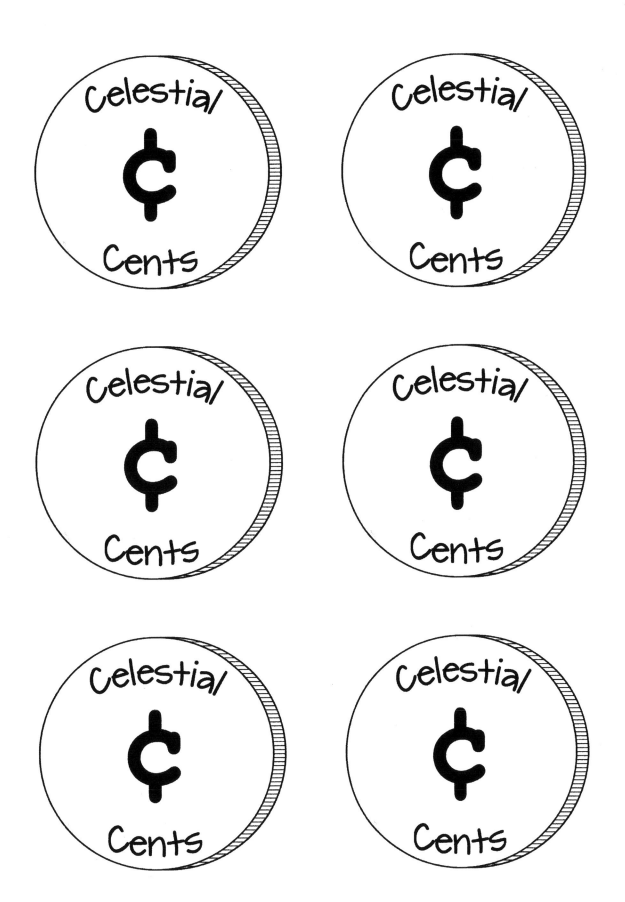

Heavenly Treasure

And whoso treasureth up my word, shall not be deceived, for the Son of Man shall come, and he shall send his angels before him with the great sound of a trumpet, and they shall gather together the remainder of his elect from the four winds, from one end of heaven to the other.
(JS-M 1:37)

Behold, the field is white already to harvest; therefore, whoso desireth to reap, let him thrust in his sickle with his might, and reap while the day lasts, that he may treasure up for his soul everlasting salvation in the kingdom of God.
(D&C 6:3)

And all saints who remember to keep and do these sayings, walking in obedience to the commandments, shall receive health in their navel and marrow to their bones; And shall find wisdom and great treasures of knowledge, even hidden treasures.
(D&C 89:18–19)

Now therefore, if ye will obey my voice indeed, and keep my covenant, then ye shall be a peculiar treasure unto me above all people: for all the earth is mine.
(Exodus 19:5)

The Lord shall open unto thee his good treasure, the heaven to give the rain unto thy land in his season, and to bless all the work of thine hand: and thou shalt lend unto many nations, and thou shalt not borrow.
(Deuteronomy 28:12)

The Lord is exalted; for he dwelleth on high: he hath filled Zion with judgment and righteousness. And wisdom and knowledge shall be the stability of thy times, and strength of salvation: the fear of the Lord is his treasure.
(Isaiah 33:5–6)

Pray always, and I will pour out my Spirit upon you, and great shall be your blessing—yea, even more than if you should obtain treasures of earth and corruptibleness to the extent thereof.
(D&C 19:38)

Hearken ye to these words. Behold, I am Jesus Christ, the Savior of the world. Treasure these things up in your hearts, and let the solemnities of eternity rest upon your minds.
(D&C 43:34)

Let the word of Christ dwell in you richly in all wisdom; teaching and admonishing one another in psalms and hymns and spiritual songs, singing with grace in your hearts to the Lord.
(Colossians 3:16)

Are not two sparrows sold for a farthing? and one of them shall not fall on the ground without your Father. But the very hairs of your head are all numbered. Fear ye not therefore, ye are of more value than many sparrows.
(Matthew 10:29–31)

And [Jesus] found in the temple those that sold oxen and sheep and doves, and the changers of money sitting: And when he had made a scourge of small cords, he drove them all out of the temple, and the sheep, and the oxen; and poured out the changers' money, and overthrew the tables.
(John 2:14–15)

[The Nephites] Having been visited by the Spirit of God; having conversed with angels, and having been spoken unto by the voice of the Lord; and having the spirit of prophecy, and the spirit of revelation, and also many gifts, the gift of speaking with tongues, and the gift of preaching, and the gift of the Holy Ghost, and the gift of translation . . . And now behold I say unto you, that . . . this people . . . have received so many blessings from the hand of the Lord.
(Alma 9:21–23)

And there came a certain poor widow, and she threw in two mites, which make a farthing. And he called unto him his disciples, and saith unto them, Verily I say unto you, That this poor widow hath cast more in, than all they which have cast into the treasury: For all they did cast in of their abundance; but she of her want did cast in all that she had, even all her living.
(Mark 12:42–44)

In the house of the righteous is much treasure: but in the revenues of the wicked is trouble.
(Proverbs 15:6)

And, if you keep my commandments and endure to the end you shall have eternal life, which gift is the greatest of all the gifts of God.
(D&C 14:7)

And now, behold, I say unto you, that the thing which will be of the most worth unto you will be to declare repentance unto this people, that you may bring souls unto me, that you may rest with them in the kingdom of my Father.
(D&C 15:6)

Remember the worth of souls is great in the sight of God.
(D&C 18:10)

And we had obtained the records which the Lord had commanded us, and searched them and found that they were desirable; yea, even of great worth unto us, insomuch that we could preserve the commandments of the Lord unto our children.
(1 Nephi 5:21)

APRIL
THE ATONEMENT

Objective: To help family members more fully understand the role of Jesus Christ in fulfilling the Atonement.

Supplies Needed: One picture of the resurrected Savior measuring 9" x 11" on cardstock paper. Free pictures can be printed using the Gospel Art Kit pictures available on LDS.org on the Internet. An enlarged copy of a picture from the *Ensign* would also work well.

Directions: Copy the puzzle pages and then cut off the margins. When fit together as one, the puzzle should measure 9" x 11". Glue the puzzle pages to the back of the picture of the Savior. Laminate the picture puzzle for durability, then cut apart the individual pieces.

Lesson: Place all of the puzzle pieces on a table or display surface, picture side up (or in plastic eggs for an Easter lesson). Begin the lesson by giving a brief explanation of the Atonement—Christ's suffering in the Garden of Gethsemane, His death on the cross, and His eventual resurrection. The Atonement enables us to return to live again with Heavenly Father. Tell family members that the prophet Nephi in the Book of Mormon taught that "all the holy prophets" have testified of Christ's Atonement (see Helaman 8:16). Begin reading some of these testimonies by having a family member select one puzzle piece. Read the scripture and discuss its importance in relation to the atonement of the Savior. Gradually read all of the scriptures and put the pieces together one at a time to complete the picture. Display the puzzle picture in your home throughout the month as a visual reminder.

Activity: Have family members create personal picture books to look at during the sacrament. Collect pictures of the Savior, His atoning sacrifice, and His life on earth from old copies of the *Ensign* or *Friend.* Have family members choose their favorite pictures to place in their books. Copies of the sacrament prayers, pictures of latter-day prophets, temples, or other meaningful pictures may also be included if desired.

SCRIPTURES

Isaiah 25:8	2 Nephi 2:6	3 Nephi 11:11
Isaiah 53:5	Mosiah 3:17	3 Nephi 11:14
Matthew 1:21	Mosiah 14:4	Mormon 9:12
John 3:17	Mosiah 16:15	Moroni 7:41
1 Corinthians 15:22	Alma 7:13	Moroni 10:33
Hebrews 5:9	Alma 11:40	D&C 18:11
1 John 2:2	Alma 42:15	Moses 1:6
1 John 4:14	Helaman 5:9	Moses 1:39
1 Nephi 10:4	Helaman 14:15	Articles of Faith 1:3
Hebrews 9:12	Alma 34:8	D&C 20:21–25

ADDITIONAL RESOURCES:

Music: "I Lived in Heaven" (*Children's Songbook*, 4); "He Sent His Son" (*Children's Songbook*, 34); "Come Follow Me" (*Hymns*, no. 116).

Story: Meghan Decker, "Parable of the Ketchup," *Friend*, Apr. 1999, 32

Quote: "Those who will receive the Lord Jesus Christ as the source of their salvation will always lie down in green pastures, no matter how barren and bleak the winter has been. And the waters of their refreshment will always be still waters, no matter how turbulent the storms of life. In walking His path of righteousness, our souls will be forever restored; and though that path may for us, as it did for Him, lead through the very valley of the shadow of death, yet we will fear no evil. The rod of His priesthood and the staff of His Spirit will always comfort us," (Jeffrey R. Holland, " 'He Hath Filled the Hungry with Good Things,' " Ensign, Nov. 1997, 64).;

Suggested Treat: Rice Krispie treats shaped like Easter eggs.

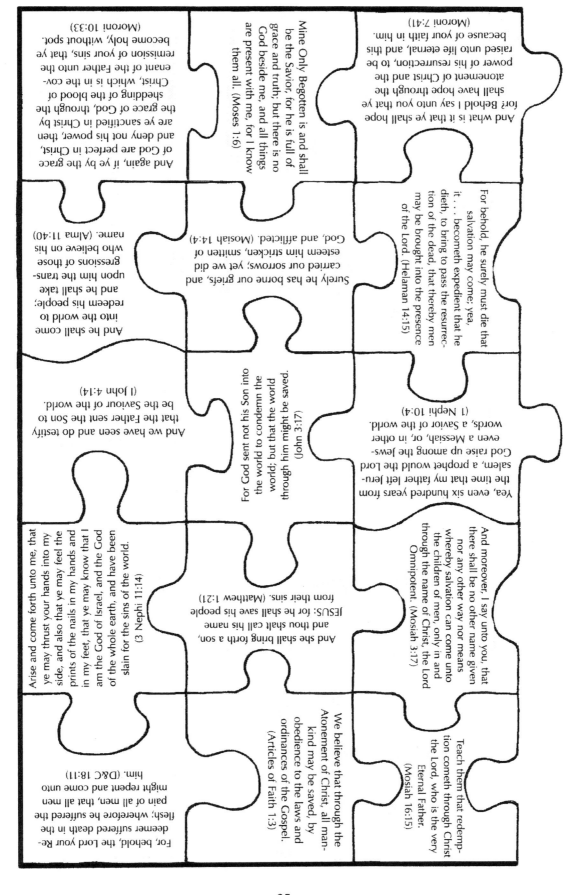

And what is it that ye shall hope for? Behold I say unto you that ye shall have hope through the atonement of Christ and the power of his resurrection, to be raised unto life eternal, and this because of your faith in him. (Moroni 7:41)

Mine Only Begotten is and shall be the Savior, for he is full of grace and truth; but there is no God beside me, and all things are present with me, for I know them all. (Moses 1:6)

And again, if ye by the grace of God are perfect in Christ, and deny not his power, then are ye sanctified in Christ by the grace of God, through the shedding of the blood of Christ, which is in the covenant of the Father unto the remission of your sins, that ye become holy, without spot. (Moroni 10:33)

For behold, he surely must die that salvation may come; yea, it . . . becometh expedient that he dieth, to bring to pass the resurrection of the dead, that thereby men may be brought into the presence of the Lord. (Helaman 14:15)

Surely he has borne our griefs, and carried our sorrows; yet we did esteem him stricken, smitten of God, and afflicted. (Mosiah 14:4)

And he shall come into the world to redeem his people; and he shall take upon him the transgressions of those who believe on his name. (Alma 11:40)

And we have seen and do testify that the Father sent the Son to be the Saviour of the world. (1 John 4:14)

For God sent not his Son into the world to condemn the world; but that the world through him might be saved. (John 3:17)

Yea, even six hundred years from the time that my father left Jerusalem, a prophet would the Lord God raise up among the Jews—even a Messiah, or, in other words, a Savior of the world. (1 Nephi 10:4)

Arise and come forth unto me, that ye may thrust your hands into my side, and also that ye may feel the prints of the nails in my hands and in my feet, that ye may know that I am the God of Israel, and the God of the whole earth, and have been slain for the sins of the world. (3 Nephi 11:14)

And she shall bring forth a son, and thou shalt call his name JESUS: for he shall save his people from their sins. (Matthew 1:21)

And moreover, I say unto you, that there shall be no other name given nor any other way nor means whereby salvation can come unto the children of men, only in and through the name of Christ, the Lord Omnipotent. (Mosiah 3:17)

For, behold, the Lord your Redeemer suffered death in the flesh; wherefore he suffered the pain of all men, that all men might repent and come unto him. (D&C 18:11)

We believe that through the Atonement of Christ, all mankind may be saved, by obedience to the laws and ordinances of the Gospel. (Articles of Faith 1:3)

Teach them that redemption cometh through Christ the Lord, who is the very Eternal Father. (Mosiah 16:15)

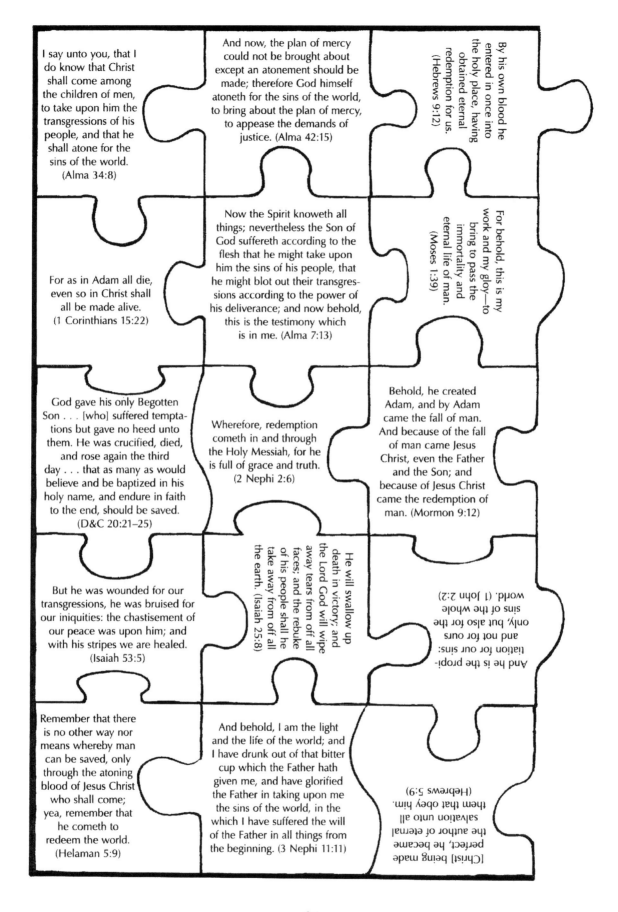

I say unto you, that I do know that Christ shall come among the children of men, to take upon him the transgressions of his people, and that he shall atone for the sins of the world. (Alma 34:8)

And now, the plan of mercy could not be brought about except an atonement should be made; therefore God himself atoneth for the sins of the world, to bring about the plan of mercy, to appease the demands of justice. (Alma 42:15)

By his own blood he entered in once into the holy place, having obtained eternal redemption for us. (Hebrews 9:12)

For as in Adam all die, even so in Christ shall all be made alive. (1 Corinthians 15:22)

Now the Spirit knoweth all things; nevertheless the Son of God suffereth according to the flesh that he might take upon him the sins of his people, that he might blot out their transgressions according to the power of his deliverance; and now behold, this is the testimony which is in me. (Alma 7:13)

For behold, this is my work and my glory—to bring to pass the immortality and eternal life of man. (Moses 1:39)

God gave his only Begotten Son . . . [who] suffered temptations but gave no heed unto them. He was crucified, died, and rose again the third day . . . that as many as would believe and be baptized in his holy name, and endure in faith to the end, should be saved. (D&C 20:21–25)

Wherefore, redemption cometh in and through the Holy Messiah, for he is full of grace and truth. (2 Nephi 2:6)

Behold, he created Adam, and by Adam came the fall of man. And because of the fall of man came Jesus Christ, even the Father and the Son; and because of Jesus Christ came the redemption of man. (Mormon 9:12)

But he was wounded for our transgressions, he was bruised for our iniquities: the chastisement of our peace was upon him; and with his stripes we are healed. (Isaiah 53:5)

He will swallow up death in victory; and the Lord God will wipe away tears from off all faces; and the rebuke of his people shall he take away from off all the earth. (Isaiah 25:8)

And he is the propitiation for our sins: and not for ours only, but also for the sins of the whole world. (1 John 2:2)

Remember that there is no other way nor means whereby man can be saved, only through the atoning blood of Jesus Christ who shall come; yea, remember that he cometh to redeem the world. (Helaman 5:9)

And behold, I am the light and the life of the world; and I have drunk out of that bitter cup which the Father hath given me, and have glorified the Father in taking upon me the sins of the world, in the which I have suffered the will of the Father in all things from the beginning. (3 Nephi 11:11)

[Christ] being made perfect, he became the author of eternal salvation unto all them that obey him. (Hebrews 5:9)

MAY

MOTHER'S DAY

Objective: To help family members gain a greater appreciation for mothers in celebration of Mother's Day.

Supplies Needed: 31 green pipe cleaners and a vase.

Directions: Copy the rose page three times onto colored cardstock paper. Cut out the scripture circles and the roses. Attach the scripture circles to the back of the roses. Laminate the scripture roses for durability, if desired. Attach a green pipe cleaner to each scripture rose as a stem. Have the vase on hand for use during the lesson.

Lesson: Review with family members the importance of women, especially mothers, in Heavenly Father's plan. Brainstorm with family members some of the many things mothers do to make family life better. Take turns reading the scripture roses and discussing their importance. Place the scripture roses in the vase after each has been read. Display the bouquet of scripture roses throughout the month as a visual reminder to show gratitude for mothers.

Activity: Take time to teach family members about grandmothers (including great-grandmothers) with whom they may not be familiar. Show pictures, read journal entries, and look at other meaningful family mementos that serve as reminders of these women. Tell about the sacrifices these women made as mothers to help serve their families.

SCRIPTURES

Genesis 3:20	Ezekiel 19:2	2 Timothy 1:5
Genesis 7:16	Ezekiel 19:10	Mosiah 3:8
Genesis 17:16	Isaiah 49:1	Alma 56:47–48
Exodus 20:12	Isaiah 66:13	Alma 57:21
Proverbs 1:8	Luke 2:19	D&C 138:39
Proverbs 23:25	John 19:26–27	Moses 5:11

ADDITIONAL RESOURCES:

Music: "I Often Go Walking" (*Children's Songbook*, 202); "Mother, I Love You" (*Children's Songbook*, 207); "As Sisters in Zion" (*Hymns*, no. 309).

Story: Alma J. Yates, "Roses Twice," *New Era*, May 1984, 44

Quote: "There is no role in life more essential and more eternal than that of motherhood," (M. Russell Ballard, "Daughters of God," *Ensign*, May 2008, 108–10).

Suggested Treat: Chocolate roses

But Mary kept all these things, and pondered them in her heart. (Luke 2:19)

When Jesus therefore saw his mother, and the disciple standing by, whom he loved, he saith unto his mother, Woman, behold thy son! Then saith he to the disciple, Behold thy mother! And from that hour that disciple took her unto his own home. (John 19:26–27)

Now they never had fought, yet they did not fear death; and they did think more upon the liberty of their fathers than they did upon their lives; yea, they had been taught by their mothers, that if they did not doubt, God would deliver them. And they rehearsed unto me the words of their mothers, saying: We do not doubt our mothers knew it. (Alma 56:47–48)

Thy father and thy mother shall be glad, and she that bare thee shall rejoice. (Proverbs 23:25)

Yea, and they did obey and observe to perform every word of command with exactness; yea, and even according to their faith it was done unto them; and I did remember the words which they said unto me that their mothers had taught them. (Alma 57:21)

And our glorious Mother Eve, with many of her faithful daughters who had lived through the ages and worshiped the true and living God. (D&C 138:39)

And Eve, his wife, heard all these things and was glad, saying: Were it not for our transgression we never should have had seed, and never should have known good and evil, and the joy of our redemption, and the eternal life which God giveth unto all the obedient. (Moses 5:11)

And they that went in, went in male and female of all flesh, as God had commanded him: and the Lord shut him in. (Genesis 7:16)

Listen, O isles, unto me; and hearken, ye people, from far; The Lord hath called me from the womb; from the bowels of my mother hath he made mention of my name. (Isaiah 49:1)

Thy mother is like a vine in thy blood, planted by the waters: she was fruitful and full of branches by reason of many waters. (Ezekiel 19:10)

What is thy mother? A lioness: she lay down among lions, she nourished her whelps among young lions. (Ezekiel 19:2)

And Adam called his wife's name Eve; because she was the mother of all living. (Genesis 3:20)

And I will bless her, and give thee a son also of her: yea, I will bless her, and she shall be a mother of nations; kings of people shall be of her.
(Genesis 17:16)

Honour thy father and thy mother: that thy days may be long upon the land which the Lord thy God giveth thee.
(Exodus 20:12)

My son, hear the instruction of thy father, and forsake not the law of thy mother.
(Proverbs 1:8)

As one whom his mother comforteth, so will I comfort you; and ye shall be comforted in Jerusalem.
(Isaiah 66:13)

When I call to remembrance the unfeigned faith that is in thee, which dwelt first in thy grandmother Lois, and thy mother Eunice; and I am persuaded that in thee also.
(2 Timothy 1:5)

And he shall be called Jesus Christ, the Son of God, the Father of heaven and earth, the Creator of all things from the beginning; and his mother shall be called Mary.
(Mosiah 3:8)

JUNE

FATHER'S DAY

Objective: To help family members gain a greater appreciation for fathers and father figures.

Directions: Cut out and color the five different pictures of fathers on the following pages. Cut out the scripture cards. Laminate the pictures and scriptures for durability, if desired. Attach the pictures of fathers to a display surface, leaving room below the pictures for the scripture cards.

Lesson: Show family members the five different pictures of fathers, and briefly explain how each meets the role of fatherhood. Explain that the scriptures mention each of these types of fathers and give us greater insight to each. Place all of the scriptures in a container and randomly pull them out one at a time. Read the scripture, decide which type of father is being discussed in the scripture, then post it under the picture of the corresponding father. Display the pictures of the fathers throughout the remainder of the month as a visual reminder to show gratitude for fathers.

Activity: Read the "The Family: A Proclamation to the World" as a family to gain a clear understanding of the role the father plays in the home. Discuss how family members can help support Dad in his important, but varied, family responsibilities. Have teenage boys think of what things they could do now to help themselves prepare to be fathers in the future.

SCRIPTURES

Father	Ward Father (Bishop)	Founding Father	Spiritual Father (Jesus Christ)	Heavenly Father
Proverbs 3:12	Titus 1:7	1 Nephi 13:12	Isaiah 9:6	Mosiah 2:34
Ephesians 6:4	D&C 46:27	D&C 10:49–51	Mosiah 3:8	3 Nephi 13:6
Enos 1:1	D&C 72:9–12	D&C 101:80	Alma 11:38–39	Mormon 6:22
"The Family: A Proclamation to the World" 1:7	D&C 107:68	D&C 109:54	D&C 93:3–4	Articles of Faith 1:1

ADDITIONAL RESOURCES:

Music: "Fathers" (Children's Songbook p. 209); "Daddy's Homecoming" (Children's Songbook p. 210); "O My Father" (Hymns no. 292).

Story: Sheila Kindred, "Father's Day Detective," Friend, Jun 2008, 12–13

Quote: "If the father will love God, love his wife, love his family, and honor his priesthood, he will have very little to worry about. If all the priesthood would do that throughout the world, what a great influence we would have," (N. Eldon Tanner, "Priesthood Responsibilities," Ensign, Jul 1973, 92).

Suggested Treat: Big Hunk candy bars

Founding Father

Ward Father
(Bishop)

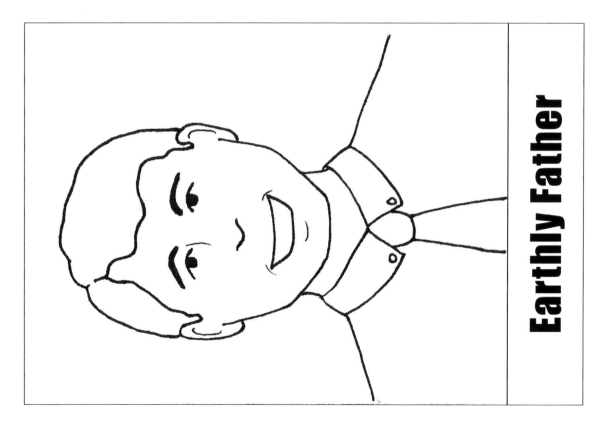

Earthly Father

Heavenly Father

Spiritual Father
(Jesus Christ)

The word of the Lord . . . making known the duty of the bishop... which is verily this— To keep the Lord's storehouse; to receive the funds of the church in this part of the vineyard; To take an account of the elders as before has been commanded; and to administer to their wants, who shall pay for that which they receive, inasmuch as they have wherewith to pay.
(D&C 72:9–12)

The office of a bishop is in administering all temporal things.
(D&C 107:68)

For a bishop must be blameless, as the steward of God; not selfwilled, not soon angry, not given to wine, no striker, not given to filthy lucre.
(Titus 1:7)

And unto the bishop of the church, and unto such as God shall appoint and ordain to watch over the church and to be elders unto the church, are to have it given unto them to discern all those gifts lest there shall be any among you professing and yet be not of God.
(D&C 46:27)

And, ye fathers, provoke not your children to wrath: but bring them up in the nurture and admonition of the Lord.
(Ephesians 6:4)

For whom the Lord loveth he correcteth; even as a father the son in whom he delighteth.
(Proverbs 3:12)

Behold, it came to pass that I, Enos, [knew] my father that he was a just man—for he taught me in his language, and also in the nurture and admonition of the Lord—and blessed be the name of my God for it.
(Enos 1:1)

By divine design, fathers are to preside over their families in love and righteousness and are responsible to provide the necessities of life and protection for their families.
("The Family: A Proclamation to the World" 1:7)

But thou, when thou prayest, enter into thy closet, and when thou hast shut thy door, pray to thy Father who is in secret; and thy Father, who seeth in secret, shall reward thee openly.
(3 Nephi 13:6)

I say unto you, that there are not any among you, except it be your little children that have not been taught concerning these things, but what knoweth that ye are eternally indebted to your heavenly Father, to render to him all that you have and are.
(Mosiah 2:34)

But behold, . . . the Father, yea, the Eternal Father of heaven, knoweth your state; and he doeth with you according to his justice and mercy.
(Mormon 6:22)

We believe in God, the Eternal Father, and in His Son, Jesus Christ, and in the Holy Ghost.
(Articles of Faith 1:1)

Now Zeezrom saith again unto him: Is the Son of God the very Eternal Father? And Amulek said unto him: Yea, he is the very Eternal Father of heaven and of earth, and all things which in them are; he is the beginning and the end, the first and the last. (Alma 11:38–39)

For unto us a child is born, unto us a son is given: and the government shall be upon his shoulder: and his name shall be called Wonderful, Counsellor, The mighty God, The everlasting Father, The Prince of Peace. (Isaiah 9:6)

And he shall be called Jesus Christ, the Son of God, the Father of heaven and earth, the Creator of all things from the beginning; and his mother shall be called Mary. (Mosiah 3:8)

And that I am in the Father, and the Father in me, and the Father and I are one—The Father because he gave me of his fulness, and the Son because I was in the world and made flesh my tabernacle, and dwelt among the sons of men. (D&C 93:3–4)

Their faith in their prayers was that this gospel should be made known also, if it were possible that other nations should possess this land; And thus they did leave a blessing upon this land in their prayers, that whosoever should believe in this gospel in this land might have eternal life; Yea, that it might be free unto all of whatsoever nation, kindred, tongue, or people they may be. (D&C 10:49–51)

And I looked and beheld a man among the Gentiles, who was separated from the seed of my brethren by the many waters; and I beheld the Spirit of God, that it came down and wrought upon the man; and he went forth upon the many waters, even unto the seed of my brethren, who were in the promised land. (1 Nephi 13:12)

And for this purpose have I established the Constitution of this land, by the hands of wise men whom I raised up unto this very purpose, and redeemed the land by the shedding of blood. (D&C 101:80)

Have mercy, O Lord, upon all the nations of the earth; have mercy upon the rulers of our land; may those principles, which were so honorably and nobly defended, namely, the Constitution of our land, by our fathers, be established forever. (D&C 109:54)

JULY

FREEDOM AND LIBERTY

Objective: Help family members understand that Heavenly Father wants His children to be free to exercise their agency and that the American continent was set aside as the promised land offering freedom and liberty to those blessed to live there.

Directions: Enlarge the flag banner page by 250 percent onto poster size paper (or make a similar flag on poster board using markers or pieced construction paper). Color the top (solid half) blue and the bottom stripes red and white. Copy the scripture stars onto white cardstock paper, and cut them out. Laminate the flag banner and the scripture stars for durability if desired.

Lesson: Teach family members that Heavenly Father places great value on the need for freedom and liberty; agency is an essential part of the plan of salvation. Heavenly Father made sure the Restoration of the gospel took place in a free land. Read about these points in the scriptures by taking turns reading a scripture star. Discuss the importance of each scripture in understanding personal or national freedom. Have family members place the scripture stars on the flag banner. Display the flag banner in your home throughout the month as a visual reminder of the importance of freedom and liberty.

Activity: Take time during family home evening to read parts of the Constitution and list some of the freedoms it specifically designates for citizens of the United States. Learn about the founding fathers and how they worked to ensure the birth of the nation was based firmly in freedom and liberty.

SCRIPTURES

John 8:32	2 Nephi 2:27	D&C 10:50–51
2 Corinthians 3:17	Mosiah 29:32	D&C 38:22
Galatians 5:1	Alma 48:11	D&C 88:86
James 1:25	Alma 61:9	D&C 98:5
James 2:12	Helaman 14:30	D&C 134:2
2 Nephi 1:7	Ether 2:12	Moses 4:3

ADDITIONAL RESOURCES

Music: "My Country" (*Children's Songbook*, 224); "My Flag, My Flag" (*Children's Songbook*, 225); "Who's on the Lord's Side?" (*Hymns*, no. 260).

Story: "Captain Moroni and the Title of Liberty," Friend, May 1994, 20

Quote: "I marvel at the miracle of America, the land which the God of Heaven long ago declared to be a land choice above all other lands.

"I love America for her great and brawny strength, I love her for her generous heart. I love her for her tremendous spiritual strengths. She is unique among the nations of the earth—in her discovery, in her birth as a nation, in her amalgamation of the races that have come to her shores, in the strength of her government, in the goodness of her people.

"God bless America, for she is His creation," (Gordon B. Hinckley, *Stand a Little Taller: Counsel and Inspiration for Each Day of the Year* [Salt Lake City, Utah: Eagle Gate, 2001], 195).

Suggested Treat: Ice cream cones with red, white, and blue sprinkles.

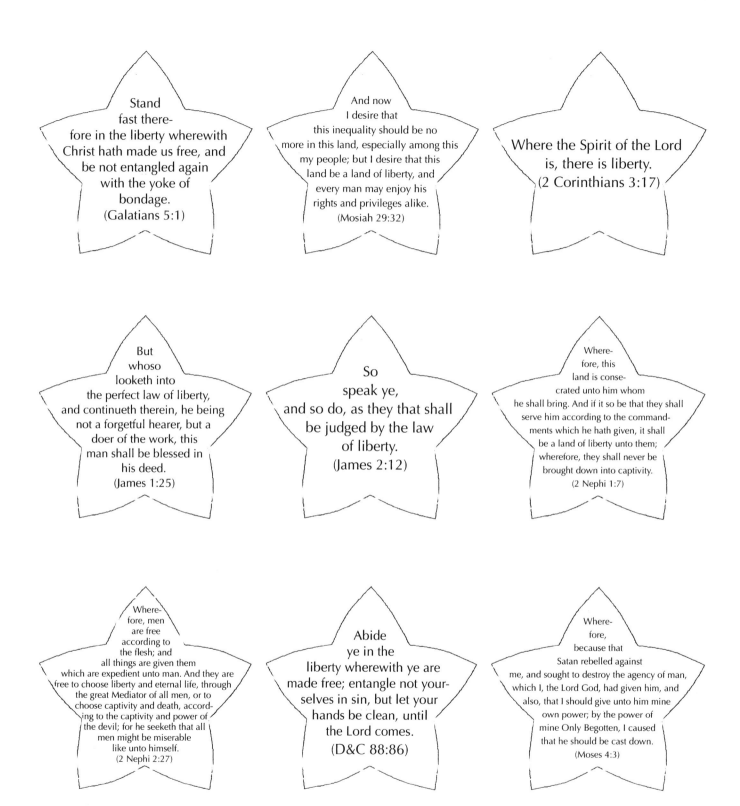

Stand fast therefore in the liberty wherewith Christ hath made us free, and be not entangled again with the yoke of bondage.
(Galatians 5:1)

And now I desire that this inequality should be no more in this land, especially among this my people; but I desire that this land be a land of liberty, and every man may enjoy his rights and privileges alike.
(Mosiah 29:32)

Where the Spirit of the Lord is, there is liberty.
(2 Corinthians 3:17)

But whoso looketh into the perfect law of liberty, and continueth therein, he being not a forgetful hearer, but a doer of the work, this man shall be blessed in his deed.
(James 1:25)

So speak ye, and so do, as they that shall be judged by the law of liberty.
(James 2:12)

Wherefore, this land is consecrated unto him whom he shall bring. And if it so be that they shall serve him according to the commandments which he hath given, it shall be a land of liberty unto them; wherefore, they shall never be brought down into captivity.
(2 Nephi 1:7)

Wherefore, men are free according to the flesh; and all things are given them which are expedient unto man. And they are free to choose liberty and eternal life, through the great Mediator of all men, or to choose captivity and death, according to the captivity and power of the devil; for he seeketh that all men might be miserable like unto himself.
(2 Nephi 2:27)

Abide ye in the liberty wherewith ye are made free; entangle not yourselves in sin, but let your hands be clean, until the Lord comes.
(D&C 88:86)

Wherefore, because that Satan rebelled against me, and sought to destroy the agency of man, which I, the Lord God, had given him, and also, that I should give unto him mine own power; by the power of mine Only Begotten, I caused that he should be cast down.
(Moses 4:3)

And Moroni was a strong and a mighty man; he was a man of a perfect understanding; yea, a man that did not delight in bloodshed; a man whose soul did joy in the liberty and the freedom of his country, and his brethren from bondage and slavery.
(Alma 48:11)

Wherefore, hear my voice and follow me, and you shall be a free people, and ye shall have no laws but my laws when I come, for I am your lawgiver, and what can stay my hand?
(D&C 38:22)

I, Pahoran, do not seek for power, save only to retain my judgment-seat that I may preserve the rights and the liberty of my people. My soul standeth fast in that liberty in the which God hath made us free.
(Alma 61:9)

And now remember, remember, my brethren, that whosoever perisheth, perisheth unto himself; and whosoever doeth iniquity, doeth it unto himself; for behold, ye are free; ye are permitted to act for yourselves; for behold, God hath given unto you a knowledge and he hath made you free.
(Helaman 14:30)

We believe that no government can exist in peace, except such laws are framed and held inviolate as will secure to each individual the free exercise of conscience, the right and control of property, and the protection of life.
(D&C 134:2)

And that law of the land which is constitutional, supporting that principle of freedom in maintaining rights and privileges, belongs to all mankind, and is justifiable before me.
(D&C 98:5)

And ye shall know the truth, and the truth shall make you free.
(John 8:32)

Behold, this is a choice land, and whatsoever nation shall possess it shall be free from bondage, and from captivity, and from all other nations under heaven, if they will but serve the God of the land, who is Jesus Christ, who hath been manifested by the things which we have written.
(Ether 2:12)

And thus they did leave a blessing upon this land in their prayers, that whosoever should believe in this gospel in this land might have eternal life; Yea, that it might be free unto all of whatsoever nation, kindred, tongue, or people they may be.
(D&C 10:50-51)

Let Freedom Ring

AUGUST
PREPARING FOR BAPTISM

Objective: To help family members understand the importance of baptism and the necessity of being baptized by one holding the priesthood.

Directions: Copy and color the Preparing for Baptism pages, placing them on a display surface joined at the dashed lines. Copy the water droplet scriptures onto a light blue cardstock paper. Cut out and laminate the scriptures for durability, if desired.

Lesson: Teach family members that baptism is the first essential ordinance required to return to live with Heavenly Father again. Learn more about the ordinance of baptism by starting with the bottom question on the Preparing for Baptism poster. Read each of the corresponding scriptures and discuss how the question is answered. After reading the scriptures, place them (words down) on the Preparing for Baptism poster over the question answered, as though the font is beginning to be filled. Continue reading the next set of scriptures to answer the second question. Repeat this process until all the questions have been answered and the font is "full." Display the Preparing for Baptism poster in your home for the month as a visual reminder of the importance of baptism.

Activity: Encourage family members who have been baptized to share their memories of this special occasion. If they have not previously done so, have them write in their journal about what they remember.

SCRIPTURES

Is baptism necessary for everyone?

Moroni 8:10–11	D&C 20:37
2 Nephi 9:23	Acts 2:38

Why should we be baptized?

2 Nephi 31:17	John 3:5
Mosiah 21:35	2 Nephi 31:5

Who can perform a baptism?

Mosiah 18:13	D&C 107:20
D&C 20:46–47	D&C 20:72–73

What is baptism for the dead?

D&C 128:18	D&C 128:13
D&C 128:12	1 Corinthians 15:39

How should baptism be performed?

D&C 20:74	3 Nephi 11:26
Articles of Faith 1:4	Mark 1:9–10

ADDITIONAL RESOURCES:

Music: "Baptism" (*Children's Songbook*, 100); "When I am Baptized" (*Children's Songbook*, 103); "Lead me into Life Eternal" (*Hymns*, no. 45).

Story: Jane McBride Choate, "Logan's Baptism," *Friend*, Jul. 2005, 28

Quote: "When we understand our baptismal covenant and the gift of the Holy Ghost, it will change our lives and will establish our total allegiance to the kingdom of God," (Robert D. Hales, "The Covenant of Baptism: To Be in the Kingdom and of the Kingdom," *Ensign*, Nov. 2000, 7).

Suggested Treat: Let family members "immerse" fruit in melted chocolate, fondue style.

Behold I say unto you that this thing shall ye teach—repentance and baptism unto those who are accountable and capable of committing sin; yea, teach parents that they must repent and be baptized, and humble themselves as their little children, and they shall all be saved with their little children. And their little children need no repentance, neither baptism. Behold, baptism is unto repentance to the fulfilling the commandments unto the remission of sins.
(Moroni 8:10–11)

And again, by way of commandment to the church concerning the manner of baptism—All those who humble themselves before God, and desire to be baptized, and come forth with broken hearts and contrite spirits, and witness before the church that they have truly repented of all their sins, and are willing to take upon them the name of Jesus Christ . . . shall be received by baptism into his church.
(D&C 20:37)

Then Peter said unto them, Repent, and be baptized every one of you in the name of Jesus Christ for the remission of sins, and ye shall receive the gift of the Holy Ghost.
(Acts 2:38)

And he commandeth all men that they must repent, and be baptized in his name, having perfect faith in the Holy One of Israel, or they cannot be saved in the kingdom of God.
(2 Nephi 9:23)

Wherefore, do the things which I have told you I have seen that your Lord and your Redeemer should do; for, for this cause have they been shown unto me, that ye might know the gate by which ye should enter. For the gate by which ye should enter is repentance and baptism by water; and then cometh a remission of your sins by fire and by the Holy Ghost.
(2 Nephi 31:17)

They were desirous to be baptized as a witness and a testimony that they were willing to serve God with all their hearts; nevertheless they did prolong the time; and an account of their baptism shall be given hereafter.
(Mosiah 21:35)

And now, if the Lamb of God, he being holy, should have need to be baptized by water, to fulfil all righteousness, O then, how much more need have we, being unholy, to be baptized, yea, even by water!
(2 Nephi 31:5)

Jesus answered, Verily, verily, I say unto thee, Except a man be born of water and of the Spirit, he cannot enter into the kingdom of God.
(John 3:5)

Then shall he immerse him or her in the water, and come forth again out of the water.
(D&C 20:74)

We believe that the first principles and ordinances of the Gospel are: first, Faith in the Lord Jesus Christ; second, Repentance; third, Baptism by immersion for the remission of sins; fourth, Laying on of hands for the gift of the Holy Ghost.
(Articles of Faith 1:4)

And then shall ye immerse them in the water, and come forth again out of the water.
(3 Nephi 11:26)

And it came to pass in those days, that Jesus came from Nazareth of Galilee, and was baptized of John in Jordan. And straightway coming up out of the water, he saw the heavens opened, and the Spirit like a dove descending upon him.
(Mark 1:9–10)

The power and authority of the lesser, or Aaronic Priesthood, is to hold the keys of the ministering of angels, and to administer in outward ordinances, the letter of the gospel, the baptism of repentance for the remission of sins, agreeable to the covenants and commandments.
(D&C 107:20)

And when he had said these words, the Spirit of the Lord was upon him, and he said: Helam, I baptize thee, having authority from the Almighty God, as a testimony that ye have entered into a covenant to serve him until you are dead as to the mortal body.
(Mosiah 18:13)

Baptism is to be administered in the following manner unto all those who repent— The person who is called of God and has authority from Jesus Christ to baptize, shall go down into the water with the person who has presented himself or herself for baptism, and shall say, calling him or her by name: Having been commissioned of Jesus Christ, I baptize you in the name of the Father, and of the Son, and of the Holy Ghost. Amen.
(D&C 20:72–73)

The priest's duty is to preach, teach, expound, exhort, and baptize, and administer the sacrament, And visit the house of each member, and exhort them to pray vocally and in secret and attend to all family duties.
(D&C 20:46–47)

Herein is glory and honor, and immortality and eternal life—The ordinance of baptism by water, to be immersed therein in order to answer to the likeness of the dead, that one principle might accord with the other; to be immersed in the water and come forth out of the water is in the likeness of the resurrection of the dead in coming forth out of their graves; hence, this ordinance was instituted to form a relationship with the ordinance of baptism for the dead, being in likeness of the dead.
(D&C 128:12)

The baptismal font was instituted as a similitude of the grave, and was commanded to be in a place underneath where the living are wont to assemble, to show forth the living and the dead, and that all things may have their likeness, and that they may accord one with another—that which is earthly conforming to that which is heavenly.
(D&C 128:13)

It is sufficient to know, in this case, that the earth will be smitten with a curse unless there is a welding link of some kind or other between the fathers and the children, upon some subject or other—and behold what is that subject? It is the baptism for the dead. For we without them cannot be made perfect; neither can they without us be made perfect.
(D&C 128:18)

Else what shall they do which are baptized for the dead, if the dead rise not at all? why are they then baptized for the dead?
(1 Corinthians 15:29)

What is baptism for the dead?

Who can perform a baptism?

How should baptism be performed?

Why should we be baptized?

Is baptism necessary for everyone?

SEPTEMBER
FAITH BINGO

Objective: To teach family members the importance of having and increasing their faith. Additionally, this month's study is designed to encourage reading from the scriptures on a daily basis.

Directions: Copy the Faith BINGO cards (five unique cards are provided) and the scripture circles onto colored paper, and cut them out. Laminate the scripture circles for durability, if desired. Assign each family member a Faith BINGO card.

Lesson: Start your family home evening with a brief explanation about the definition of faith as a belief in something that cannot be seen. Consider the passage written by Grant Von Harrison in his book *Drawing on the Powers of Heaven*: "Regarding faith, the Prophet Joseph Smith taught that: 1) '. . . as faith is the moving cause of all action in temporal concerns, so it is in spiritual;' 2) '. . . faith is not only the principle of action, but of power also,' and 3) 'Faith, then, is the first great governing principle which has power, dominion, and authority over all things' " ([Orem, UT: Keepsake Paperbacks, 1992], 1).

Explain that there are many important aspects of faith taught in the scriptures. Play Faith BINGO by placing the scriptures in a container. Randomly draw one out at a time. Call out the BINGO letter and number. Have family members mark off the space on their Faith BINGO card (use a sticker, mark with a crayon, and so forth), and then read the scripture about faith. Provide rewards for individuals who get the first BINGO, four corners, or an "X" shape.

Activity: Strive as a family to exercise your collective faith regarding a specific accomplishment (such as missionary experience, improved health of a friend or relative, and so on). Decide together as a family and pray individually and as a family for the desired achievement.

SCRIPTURES

Matthew 25:21	Alma 18:35	Moroni 7:37
Luke 17:6	Alma 32:21	Moroni 10:4
Ephesians 2:8	Alma 32:26–27	Moroni 10:7
Colossians 1:23	Alma 34:17	Moroni 10:20–21
Hebrews 11:1	Alma 44:4	D&C 8:10
James 2:14, 17	Alma 48:13	D&C 20:29
1 Nephi 7:12	Ether 12:3–4	D&C 42:14
2 Nephi 9:23	Ether 12:6	D&C 75:5
Mosiah 4:30	Ether 12:18	D&C 88:118–119
Alma 14:26	Ether 12:27	D&C 104:82

ADDITIONAL RESOURCES:

Music: "Faith" (*Children's Songbook*, 96); "I Know My Father Lives" (*Children's Songbook*, 5); "I Believe in Christ" (*Hymns*, no. 134).

Story: Shauna Gibby, "A Place to Sing and Pray: A Story of Faith," *Friend*, Aug. 2004, 42

Quote: "Increased faith is what we most need. Without it, the work would stagnate. With it, no one can stop its progress." (Gordon B. Hinckley, "The Faith to Move Mountains," *Ensign*, Nov. 2006, 82–85).

Suggested Treat: Use the comparison of faith to a seed and serve nuts or popcorn.

Faith Bingo

F	A	I	T	H
1	8	16	22	30
5	11	13	24	28
3	9	18	20	25
6	12	FREE	19	27
4	7	14	21	29
2	10	15	23	26

Faith Bingo

F	A	I	T	H
5	11	17	24	28
1	9	15	22	25
6	12	13	20	27
3	7	16	19	26
2	FREE	18	21	29
4	8	14	23	30

Faith Bingo

F A I T H

F	A	I	T	H
2	9	14	23	25
3	10	17	24	27
FREE	7	15	22	26
1	11	13	20	29
5	8	16	21	30
6	12	18	19	28

Faith Bingo

F	A	I	T	H
4	7	17	19	29
6	10	16	21	26
1	8	14	23	FREE
2	11	18	24	30
5	9	15	22	25
3	12	13	20	28

Faith Bingo

F	A	I	T	H
3	10	18	21	27
2	7	14	FREE	29
5	11	17	19	26
4	8	15	22	30
6	12	13	20	28
1	9	16	24	25

F-1

For he did cry from the morning, even until the going down of the sun, exhorting the people to believe in God unto repentance lest they should be destroyed, saying unto them that by faith all things are fulfilled— Wherefore, whoso believeth in God might with surety hope for a better world, yea, even a place at the right hand of God, which hope cometh of faith, maketh an anchor to the souls of men, which would make them sure and steadfast, always abounding in good works, being led to glorify God.
(Ether 12:3–4)

F-2

And now, I, Moroni, would speak somewhat concerning these things; I would show unto the world that faith is things which are hoped for and not seen; wherefore, dispute not because ye see not, for ye receive no witness until after the trial of your faith.
(Ether 12:6)

F-3

Now faith is the substance of things hoped for, the evidence of things not seen.
(Hebrews 11:1)

F-4

Behold I say unto you, Nay; for it is by faith that miracles are wrought; and it is by faith that angels appear and minister unto men; wherefore, if these things have ceased wo be unto the children of men, for it is because of unbelief, and all is vain.
(Moroni 7:37)

F-5

And now as I said concerning faith—faith is not to have a perfect knowledge of things; therefore if ye have faith ye hope for things which are not seen, which are true.
(Alma 32:21)

F-6

Now, as I said concerning faith—that it was not a perfect knowledge—even so it is with my words. Ye cannot know of their surety at first, unto perfection, any more than faith is a perfect knowledge. But behold, if ye will awake and arouse your faculties, even to an experiment upon my words, and exercise a particle of faith, yea, even if ye can no more than desire to believe, let this desire work in you, even until ye believe in a manner that ye can give place for a portion of my words.
(Alma 32:26–27)

A-7

And inasmuch as ye are humble and faithful and call upon my name, behold, I will give you the victory.
(D&C 104:82)

A-8

What doth it profit, my brethren, though a man say he hath faith, and have not works? can faith save him? . . . Even so faith, if it hath not works, is dead, being alone.
(James 2:14, 17)

A-9

Now ye see that this is the true faith of God; yea, ye see that God will support, and keep, and preserve us, so long as we are faithful unto him, and unto our faith, and our religion; and never will the Lord suffer that we shall be destroyed except we should fall into transgression and deny our faith.
(Alma 44:4)

A-10

And when ye shall receive these things, I would exhort you that ye would ask God, the Eternal Father, in the name of Christ, if these things are not true; and if ye shall ask with a sincere heart, with real intent, having faith in Christ, he will manifest the truth of it unto you, by the power of the Holy Ghost.
(Moroni 10:4)

A-11

Wherefore, there must be faith; and if there must be faith there must also be hope; and if there must be hope there must also be charity. And except ye have charity ye can in nowise be saved in the kingdom of God; neither can ye be saved in the kingdom of God if ye have not faith; neither can ye if ye have no hope. (Moroni 10:20–21)

A-12

Therefore may God grant unto you, my brethren, that ye may begin to exercise your faith unto repentance, that ye begin to call upon his holy name, that he would have mercy upon you.
(Alma 34:17)

I-13

But this much I can tell you, that if ye do not watch yourselves, and your thoughts, and your words, and your deeds, and observe the commandments of God, and continue in the faith of what ye have heard concerning the coming of our Lord, even unto the end of your lives, ye must perish. And now, O man, remember, and perish not.

(Mosiah 4:30)

I-14

And neither at any time hath any wrought miracles until after their faith.

(Ether 12:18)

I-15

Yea, and how is it that ye have forgotten that the Lord is able to do all things according to his will, for the children of men, if it so be that they exercise faith in him? Wherefore, let us be faithful to him.

(1 Nephi 7:12)

I-16

Deny not the power of God; for he worketh by power, according to the faith of the children of men.

(Moroni 10:7)

I-17

Remember that without faith you can do nothing; therefore ask in faith. Trifle not with these things; do not ask for that which you ought not.

(D&C 8:10)

I-18

And the Spirit shall be given unto you by the prayer of faith; and if ye receive not the Spirit ye shall not teach.

(D&C 42:14)

T-19

Yea, and he (Captain Moroni) was a man who was firm in the faith of Christ, and he had sworn with an oath to defend his people, his rights, and his country, and his religion, even to the loss of his blood.

(Alma 48:13)

T-20

And we know that all men must repent and believe on the name of Jesus Christ, and worship the Father in his name, and endure in faith on his name to the end, or they cannot be saved in the kingdom of God.

(D&C 20:29)

T-21

His lord said unto him, Well done, thou good and faithful servant: thou hast been faithful over a few things, I will make thee ruler over many things: enter thou into the joy of thy lord.

(Matthew 25:21)

T-22

Continue in the faith grounded and settled, and be not moved away from the hope of the gospel, which ye have heard, and which was preached to every creature which is under heaven.

(Colossians 1:23)

T-23

And as all have not faith, seek ye diligently and teach one another words of wisdom; yea, seek ye out of the best books words of wisdom; seek learning, even by study and also by faith. Organize yourselves; prepare every needful thing; and establish a house, even a house of prayer, a house of fasting, a house of faith, a house of learning, a house of glory, a house of order, a house of God.

(D&C 88:118–19)

T-24

And Alma cried, saying: How long shall we suffer these great afflictions, O Lord? O Lord, give us strength according to our faith which is in Christ, even unto deliverance. And they broke the cords with which they were bound; and when the people saw this, they began to flee, for the fear of destruction had come upon them.

(Alma 14:26)

H-25

And a portion of that Spirit dwelleth in me, which giveth me knowledge, and also power according to my faith and desires which are in God.
(Alma 18:35)

H-26

And he commandeth all men that they must repent, and be baptized in his name, having perfect faith in the Holy One of Israel, or they cannot be saved in the kingdom of God.
(2 Nephi 9:23)

H-27

And if men come unto me I will show unto them their weakness. I give unto men weakness that they may be humble; and my grace is sufficient for all men that humble themselves before me; for if they humble themselves before me, and have faith in me, then will I make weak things become strong unto them.
(Ether 12:27)

H-28

And thus, if ye are faithful ye shall be laden with many sheaves, and crowned with honor, and glory, and immortality, and eternal life.
(D&C 75:5)

H-29

And the Lord said, If ye had faith as a grain of mustard seed, ye might say unto this sycamine tree, Be thou plucked up by the root, and be thou planted in the sea; and it should obey you.
(Luke 17:6)

H-30

For by grace are ye saved through faith; and that not of yourselves: it is the gift of God.
(Ephesians 2:8)

OCTOBER
LAW OF THE HARVEST

Objective: To help family members learn the necessity of working diligently for the blessings we desire to receive.

Directions: Enlarge both the Pumpkin Patch Match and the jack-o'-lantern pages 250 percent onto poster size paper. Color the pumpkins and the jack-o'-lanterns; cut out the jack-o'-lanterns. Copy and cut out the scripture circles. Glue the scriptures to the back of the jack-o'-lanterns. Laminate the Pumpkin Patch Match poster and the jack-o'-lanterns for durability, if desired.

Lesson: Begin your lesson by explaining the phrase *law of the harvest* simply means that "you don't get something for nothing." Teach family members that harvest is the time when farmers gather in the bounty of the plants they have been nurturing over the past season. The Lord uses planting and harvesting phrases often in the scriptures as a way to teach various principles of the gospel. Next, begin the Pumpkin Patch Match activity by placing the jack-o'-lanterns into a container. Draw one out and read the scripture. Discuss the importance of the verse(s) and how the harvest terminology is used symbolically. Have family members determine which pumpkin the jack-o'-lantern was made from. Attach the jack-o'-lantern onto the poster over the pumpkin it matches. Continue reading the jack-o'-lantern scriptures until all the matches are made.

Activity: Learn more about the law of the harvest by planting a fall garden outside or indoors as potted plants. Teach family members the meanings of the words *sow*, *reap*, and *first fruits* as the garden flourishes.

SCRIPTURES

Exodus 23:15–16	Matthew 9:37–38	Revelation 14:18–19
Leviticus 19:9	Matthew 13:30	2 Nephi 5:11
Leviticus 23:10–11	Matthew 13:31–32	Mosiah 7:30
Psalm 126:5	John 4:35	Alma 17:13
Proverbs 3:9	John 4:36–37	Alma 32:42–43
Proverbs 11:18	1 Corinthians 15:20–21	D&C 4:4
Proverbs 25:13	2 Corinthians 9:6–7	D&C 6:33
Ecclesiastes 11:4	Galatians 6:7	D&C 56:16
Isaiah 17:4–5	James 3:18	D&C 88:98
Hosea 10:12	Revelation 14:15	D&C 101:64

ADDITIONAL RESOURCES:

Music: "A Song of Thanks" (*Children's Songbook*, 20a); "All Things Bright and Beautiful" (*Children's Songbook*, 231); "For the Beauty of the Earth" (*Hymns*, no. 92).

Story: Angel Abrea, "Obtaining Blessings," *Friend*, Oct. 1989, inside front cover

Quote: "Let me encourage you to draw close to the soil. Have your own experience in planting a garden. Then make application in your own life of this great principle of the law of the harvest," (L. Tom Perry, "The Law of the Harvest," *New Era*, Oct. 1980, 4).

Suggested Treat: Pumpkin pie or cookies

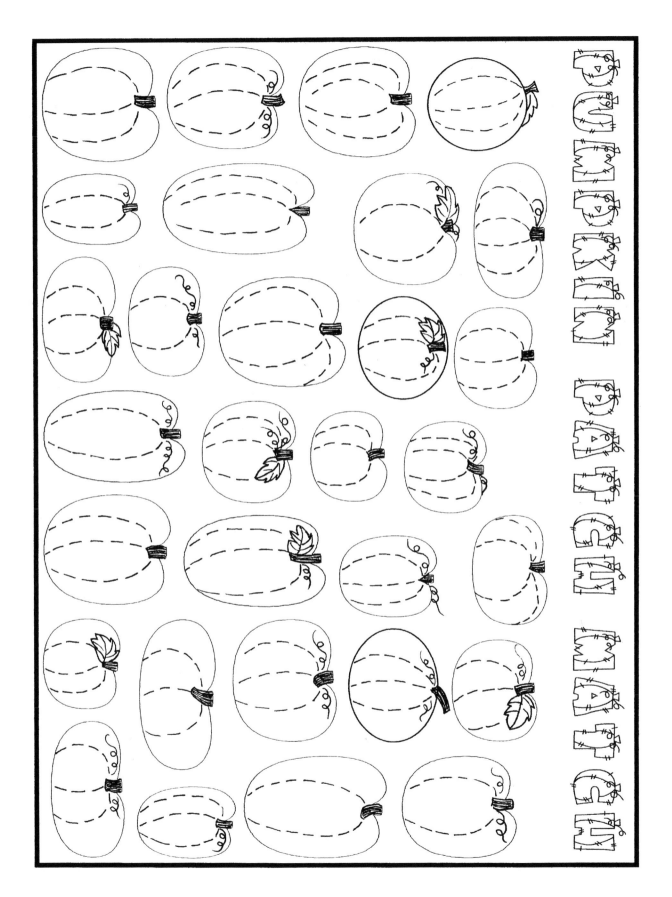

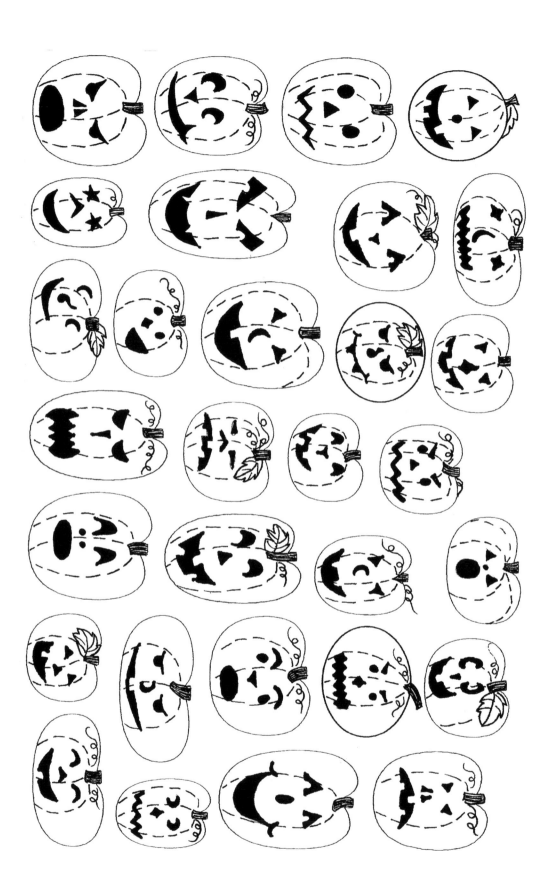

Speak unto the children of Israel, and say unto them, When ye be come into the land which I give unto you, and shall reap the harvest thereof, then ye shall bring a sheaf of the firstfruits of your harvest unto the priest: And he shall wave the sheaf before the Lord, to be accepted for you.
(Leviticus 23:10–11)

Thou shalt keep the feast of unleavened bread… And the feast of harvest, the firstfruits of thy labours, which thou hast sown in the field: and the feast of ingathering, which is in the end of the year, when thou hast gathered in thy labours out of the field.
(Exodus 23:15–16)

Honour the Lord with thy substance, and with the firstfruits of all thine increase.
(Proverbs 3:9)

But now is Christ risen from the dead, and become the firstfruits of them that slept. For since by man came death, by man came also the resurrection of the dead.
(1 Corinthians 15:20–21)

They are Christ's, the first fruits, they who shall descend with him first, and they who are on the earth and in their graves, who are first caught up to meet him; and all this by the voice of the sounding of the trump of the angel of God.
(D&C 88:98)

And when ye reap the harvest of your land, thou shalt not wholly reap the corners of thy field, neither shalt thou gather the gleanings of thy harvest.
(Leviticus 19:9)

As the cold of snow in the time of harvest, so is a faithful messenger to them that send him: for he refresheth the soul of his masters.
(Proverbs 25:13)

He that observeth the wind shall not sow; and he that regardeth the clouds shall not reap.
(Ecclesiastes 11:4)

And in that day it shall come to pass, that the glory of Jacob shall be made thin, and the fatness of his flesh shall wax lean. And it shall be as when the harvestman gathereth the corn, and reapeth the ears with his arm; and it shall be as he that gathereth ears in the valley of Rephaim.
(Isaiah 17:4–5)

Wo unto you rich men, that will not give your substance to the poor, for your riches will canker your souls; and this shall be your lamentation in the day of visitation, and of judgment, and of indignation: The harvest is past, the summer is ended, and my soul is not saved!
(D&C 56:16)

And another angel came out of the temple, crying with a loud voice to him that sat on the cloud, Thrust in thy sickle, and reap: for the time is come for thee to reap; for the harvest of the earth is ripe.
(Revelation 14:15)

Thrust in thy sharp sickle, and gather the clusters of the vine of the earth; for her grapes are fully ripe. And the angel thrust in his sickle into the earth, and gathered the vine of the earth, and cast it into the great winepress of the wrath of God.
(Revelation 14:18–19)

Then saith he unto his disciples, The harvest truly is plenteous, but the labourers are few; Pray ye therefore the Lord of the harvest, that he will send forth labourers into his harvest.
(Matthew 9:37–38)

Let both grow together until the harvest: and in the time of harvest I will say to the reapers, Gather ye together first the tares, and bind them in bundles to burn them: but gather the wheat into my barn.
(Matthew 13:30)

The kingdom of heaven is like to a grain of mustard seed, which a man took, and sowed in his field: Which indeed is the least of all seeds: but when it is grown, it is the greatest among herbs, and becometh a tree, so that the birds of the air come and lodge in the branches thereof.
(Matthew 13:31–32)

Say not ye, There are yet four months, and then cometh harvest? behold, I say unto you, Lift up your eyes, and look on the fields; for they are white already to harvest.
(John 4:35)

And he that reapeth receiveth wages, and gathereth fruit unto life eternal: that both he that soweth and he that reapeth may rejoice together. And herein is that saying true, One soweth, and another reapeth.
(John 4:36–37)

They separated themselves and departed one from another, trusting in the Lord that they should meet again at the close of their harvest; for they supposed that great was the work which they had undertaken.
(Alma 17:13)

For behold the field is white already to harvest; and lo, he that thrusteth in his sickle with his might, the same layeth up in store that he perisheth not, but bringeth salvation to his soul.
(D&C 4:4)

For the time of harvest is come, and my word must needs be fulfilled.
(D&C 101:64)

And because of your diligence and your faith and your patience with the word in nourishing it, that it may take root in you, behold, by and by ye shall pluck the fruit thereof, which is most precious, which is sweet above all that is sweet, and which is white above all that is white, yea, and pure above all that is pure; and ye shall feast upon this fruit even until ye are filled, that ye hunger not, neither shall ye thirst. Then, my brethren, ye shall reap the rewards of your faith, and your diligence, and patience, and long-suffering, waiting for the tree to bring forth fruit unto you.
(Alma 32:42–43)

And again, he saith: If my people shall sow filthiness they shall reap the chaff thereof in the whirlwind; and the effect thereof is poison.
(Mosiah 7:30)

Be not deceived; God is not mocked: for whatsoever a man soweth, that shall he also reap.
(Galatians 6:7)

Fear not to do good, my sons, for whatsoever ye sow, that shall ye also reap; therefore, if ye sow good ye shall also reap good for your reward.
(D&C 6:33)

But this I say, He which soweth sparingly shall reap also sparingly; and he which soweth bountifully shall reap also bountifully. Every man according as he purposeth in his heart, so let him give; not grudgingly, or of necessity: for God loveth a cheerful giver. (2 Corinthians 9:6–7)

Sow to yourselves in righteousness, reap in mercy; break up your fallow ground: for it is time to seek the Lord, till he come and rain righteousness upon you. (Hosea 10:12)

They that sow in tears shall reap in joy. (Psalm 126:5)

The wicked worketh a deceitful work: but to him that soweth righteousness shall be a sure reward. (Proverbs 11:18)

And the fruit of righteousness is sown in peace of them that make peace. (James 3:18)

And the Lord was with us; and we did prosper exceedingly; for we did sow seed, and we did reap again in abundance. And we began to raise flocks, and herds, and animals of every kind. (2 Nephi 5:11)

NOVEMBER
FEAST UPON THE WORD

Objective: To help family members better understand Nephi's admonition to "feast upon the word" and its relation to scripture study.

Directions: Copy the Pilgrims and Indians pages two times each. Color the Pilgrims and Indians and cut them out along the rectangle outlines. Copy the scripture verses, cut them out, and attach them to the back of the Pilgrims and Indians. On the extra Pilgrims and Indians write the words, "One of my favorite scripture stories is . . ." Copy and color the three sections of the feast table. Cut out the table sections and attach them together to form one long table. Laminate the Pilgrims, Indians, and table for durability, if desired. Place the feast table on a display surface.

Lesson: Teach family members about feasting upon the word by comparing eating at a feast to snacking. Explain that the Lord wants us to feast on his words, not just snack or nibble. Begin your family study by randomly selecting one of the Pilgrim or Indian pieces. If it has a scripture on the back, read it and discuss its importance and meaning. If it has the phrase "One of my favorite scripture stories is . . ." the person selecting should take time to share a favorite scripture story. Have a family member place the Pilgrim or Indian at the feast table by slipping it behind the table and fastening it in place. Continue selecting Pilgrims or Indians until all have been read. Display the Pilgrims and Indians at their feast table throughout the month as a visual reminder of the importance to feast upon the scriptures.

Activity: Use Gospel Art Kit pictures of scripture stories to make a matching game to play. Match pictures to story names for an easier version. Or match pictures to books of scripture, prophet names, or actual scriptural phrases for a more challenging matching game.

SCRIPTURES:

Deuteronomy 6:7	1 Nephi 15:25	D&C 1:37
Deuteronomy 8:3	2 Nephi 4:15	D&C 18:4
John 5:39	2 Nephi 31:20	D&C 26:1
Romans 15:4	2 Nephi 32:3	D&C 88:118
Revelation 1:3	Alma 17:2	Joseph Smith—Matthew 1:37
1 Nephi 5:10	Moroni 10:3	Joseph Smith—History 1:12

ADDITIONAL RESOURCES:

Music: "Scripture Power" (Clive Romney, "Scripture Power," *Friend*, Oct. 1987, 10–11); "Search, Ponder, and Pray" (*Children's Songbook*, 109); "The Iron Rod" (*Hymns*, no. 274).

Story: Annette Bay Pimentel, "Benjamin's Name," *Friend*, Jul. 2008, 14–16

Quote: "Knowledge, both temporal and spiritual, comes in steps. My testimony grew line upon line, precept upon precept, here a little, there a little (see Isaiah 28:10)—the way it does for almost all members of the Church. As a boy, I recall my mother reading Book of Mormon and Church history stories to me. I felt a sweet, peaceful, reassuring feeling that what I was learning was true. This feeling developed into a sincere desire to learn more by studying the scriptures. Nothing has had a greater impact upon my life than reading, studying, and searching the scriptures in order to gain more knowledge and intelligence," (Kimberly Webb and David A. Bednar, "The Glory of God Is Intelligence," *Friend*, Oct. 2007, 6–7).

Suggested Treat: Let family members feast on banana splits of their own creation.

Feast Upon the Word

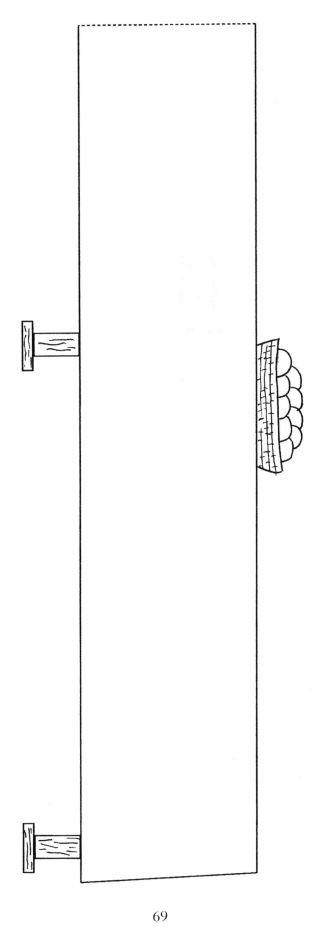

69

Behold, I say unto you that you shall let your time be devoted to the studying of the scriptures, and to preaching.
(D&C 26:1)

Search the scriptures; for in them ye think ye have eternal life: and they are they which testify of me.
(John 5:39)

And he humbled thee, and suffered thee to hunger, and fed thee with manna, which thou knewest not, neither did thy fathers know; that he might make thee know that man doth not live by bread only, but by every word that proceedeth out of the mouth of the Lord doth man live.
(Deuteronomy 8:3)

For whatsoever things were written aforetime were written for our learning, that we through patience and comfort of the scriptures might have hope.
(Romans 15:4)

Blessed is he that readeth, and they that hear the words of this prophecy, and keep those things which are written therein: for the time is at hand.
(Revelation 1:3)

For my soul delighteth in the scriptures, and my heart pondereth them, and writeth them for the learning and the profit of my children.
(2 Nephi 4:15)

Angels speak by the power of the Holy Ghost; wherefore, they speak the words of Christ. Wherefore, I said unto you, feast upon the words of Christ; for behold, the words of Christ will tell you all things what ye should do.
(2 Nephi 32:3)

Alma did rejoice exceedingly to see his brethren; and what added more to his joy, they were still his brethren in the Lord; yea, and they had waxed strong in the knowledge of the truth; for they were men of a sound understanding and they had searched the scriptures diligently, that they might know the word of God.
(Alma 17:2)

Search these commandments, for they are true and faithful, and the prophecies and promises which are in them shall all be fulfilled.
(D&C 1:37)

And as all have not faith, seek ye diligently and teach one another words of wisdom; yea, seek ye out of the best books words of wisdom; seek learning, even by study and also by faith.
(D&C 88:118)

And whoso treasureth up my word, shall not be deceived, for the Son of Man shall come, and he shall send his angels before him with the great sound of a trumpet, and they shall gather together the remainder of his elect from the four winds, from one end of heaven to the other.
(Joseph Smith—Matthew 1:37)

Never did any passage of scripture come with more power to the heart of man than this did at this time to mine. It seemed to enter with great force into every feeling of my heart. I reflected on it again and again, knowing that if any person needed wisdom from God, I did; for how to act I did not know.
(Joseph Smith—History 1:12)

Behold, I would exhort you that when ye shall read these things, if it be wisdom in God that ye should read them, that ye would remember how merciful the Lord hath been unto the children of men, from the creation of Adam even down until the time that ye shall receive these things, and ponder it in your hearts.
(Moroni 10:3)

And after they had given thanks unto the God of Israel, my father, Lehi, took the records which were engraven upon the plates of brass, and he did search them from the beginning.
(1 Nephi 5:10)

For in [the scriptures] are all things written concerning the foundation of my church, my gospel, and my rock.
(D&C 18:4)

Wherefore, ye must press forward with a steadfastness in Christ, having a perfect brightness of hope, and a love of God and of all men. Wherefore, if ye shall press forward, feasting upon the word of Christ, and endure to the end, behold, thus saith the Father: Ye shall have eternal life.
(2 Nephi 31:20)

And thou shalt teach [the scriptures] diligently unto thy children, and shalt talk of them when thou sittest in thine house, and when thou walkest by the way, and when thou liest down, and when thou risest up.
(Deuteronomy 6:7)

Wherefore, I, Nephi, did exhort them to give heed unto the word of the Lord; yea, I did exhort them with all the energies of my soul, and with all the faculty which I possessed, that they would give heed to the word of God and remember to keep his commandments always in all things.
(1 Nephi 15:25)

DECEMBER

JOURNEY TO BETHLEHEM

Objective: To teach family members the details of the events surrounding the birth of the Savior in Bethlehem, as well as to review happenings that occurred on the American continent.

Directions: Copy the three panels of the Journey to Bethlehem map, the picture of Mary and Joseph below, and the scripture cheat-sheet pages. Cut out and color the three sections of the Journey to Bethlehem map; attach the three sections together to form the map. Laminate the map and Mary and Joseph for durability, if desired. Place the map on a display surface with Mary and Joseph on the first stepping stone by Nazareth.

Lesson: Reenact the story of the birth of the Savior as told in the New Testament by reading the scriptures (1 through 24) on the cheat sheet. While reading each verse, gradually move Mary and Joseph closer to Bethlehem along the path of stepping stones. Take time to discuss the importance and impact of these verses. Then reenact the story of Christ's birth and the signs seen on the American continent (25 through 30), continuing to move Mary and Joseph along the path with each verse. At the end, read the final verse from Isaiah (31). Take time to share testimonies of the Savior and express gratitude for his birth and life on this earth. Display the Journey to Bethlehem map throughout the month as a visual reminder of the importance of the Christmas season.

Activity: Sing or play Christmas carols about the birth of the Savior that complement the scripture verses read.

SCRIPTURES

Luke 2:1, 3	Luke 2:10	Luke 2:16	Matthew 2:3-4	Matthew 2:10
Luke 2:4–5	Luke 2:11	Luke 2:17	Matthew 2:5	Matthew 2:11
Luke 2:6	Luke 2:12	Luke 2:18–19	Matthew 2:7	Matthew 2:12
Luke 2:7	Luke 2:13–14	Matthew 2:1	Matthew 2:8	Isaiah 9:6
Luke 2:8	Luke 2:15	Matthew 2:2	Matthew 2:9	3 Nephi 1:5–6
Luke 2:9	3 Nephi 1:9–10	3 Nephi 1:11–13	3 Nephi 1:14	3 Nephi 1:15–16
3 Nephi 1:19–20				

ADDITIONAL RESOURCES:

Music: "Away in a Manger" (*Children's Songbook*, 42); "Once Within a Lowly Stable" (*Children's Songbook*, 41); "Angels We Have Heard on High" (*Hymns*, no. 203).

Story: Charlotte McEwan, "The Secret Giver," *Friend*, Dec. 2008, 4–6

Quote: "As we seek Christ, as we find Him, as we follow Him, we shall have the Christmas spirit. . . . We shall learn to forget ourselves. We shall turn our thoughts to the greater benefit of others," (Thomas S. Monson, "In Search of the Christmas Spirit," *Ensign*, Dec. 1987, 5).

Suggested Treat: Star-shaped frosted sugar cookies

Journey to Bethlehem

Nazareth

1

2

3

4

5

6

7

8

9

N

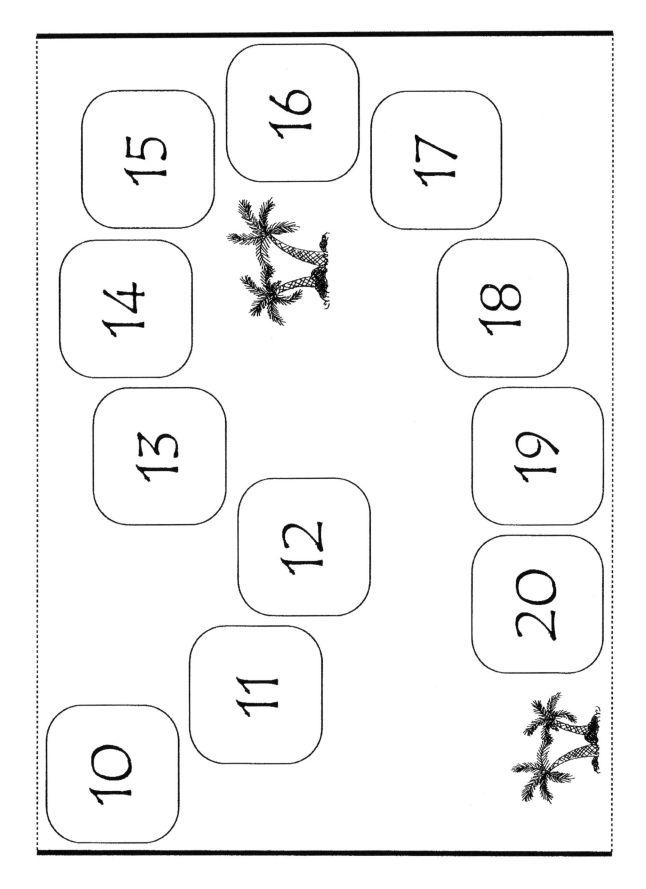

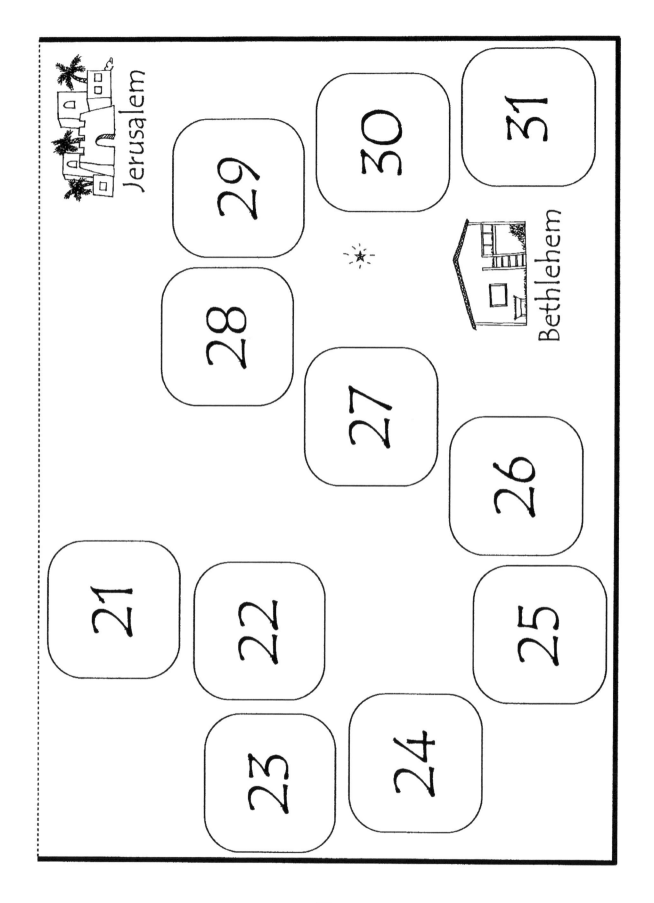

78

Scripture Cheat Sheet

1: And it came to pass in those days, that there went out a decree from Caesar Augustus, that all the world should be taxed. And all went to be taxed, every one into his own city. (Luke 2:1, 3)

2: And Joseph also went up from Galilee, out of the city of Nazareth, into Judaea, unto the city of David, which is called Bethlehem; To be taxed with Mary his espoused wife, being great with child. (Luke 2:4–5)

3: And so it was, that, while they were there, the days were accomplished that she should be delivered. (Luke 2:6)

4: And she brought forth her firstborn son, and wrapped him in swaddling clothes, and laid him in a manger; because there was no room for them in the inn. (Luke 2:7)

5: And there were in the same country shepherds abiding in the field, keeping watch over their flock by night. (Luke 2:8)

6: And, lo, the angel of the Lord came upon them, and the glory of the Lord shone round about them: and they were sore afraid. (Luke 2:9)

7: And the angel said unto them, Fear not: for, behold, I bring you good tidings of great joy, which shall be to all people. (Luke 2:10)

8: For unto you is born this day in the city of David a Saviour, which is Christ the Lord. (Luke 2:11)

9: And this shall be a sign unto you; Ye shall find the babe wrapped in swaddling clothes, lying in a manger. (Luke 2:12)

10: And suddenly there was with the angel a multitude of the heavenly host praising God, and saying, Glory to God in the highest, and on earth peace, good will toward men. (Luke 2:13–14)

11: And it came to pass, as the angels were gone away from them into heaven, the shepherds said one to another, Let us now go even unto Bethlehem, and see this thing which is come to pass, which the Lord hath made known unto us. (Luke 2:15)

12: And they came with haste, and found Mary, and Joseph, and the babe lying in a manger. (Luke 2:16)

13: And when they had seen it, they made known abroad the saying which was told them concerning this child. (Luke 2:17)

14: And all they that heard it wondered at those things which were told them by the shepherds. But Mary kept all these things, and pondered them in her heart. (Luke 2:18–19)

15: Now when Jesus was born in Bethlehem of Judaea in the days of Herod the king, behold, there came wise men from the east to Jerusalem. (Matthew 2:1)

16: Saying, Where is he that is born King of the Jews? for we have seen his star in the east, and are come to worship him. (Matthew 2:2)

17: When Herod the king had heard these things, he was troubled, and all Jerusalem with him. And when he had gathered all the chief priests and scribes of the people together, he demanded of them where Christ should be born. (Matthew 2:3–4)

18: And they said unto him, In Bethlehem of Judaea: for thus it is written by the prophet. (Matthew 2:5)

19: Then Herod, when he had privily called the wise men, enquired of them diligently what time the star appeared. (Matthew 2:7)

20: And he sent them to Bethlehem, and said, Go and search diligently for the young child; and when ye have found him, bring me word again, that I may come and worship him also. (Matthew 2:8)

21: When they had heard the king, they departed; and, lo, the star, which they saw in the east, went before them, till it came and stood over where the young child was. (Matthew 2:9)

22: When they saw the star, they rejoiced with exceeding great joy. (Matthew 2:10)

23: And when they were come into the house, they saw the young child with Mary his mother, and fell down, and worshipped him: and when they had opened their treasures, they presented unto him gifts; gold, and frankincense, and myrrh. (Matthew 2:11)

24: And being warned of God in a dream that they should not return to Herod, they departed into their own country another way. (Matthew 2:12)

25: There were some who began to say that the time was past for the words to be fulfilled, which were spoken by Samuel, the Lamanite. And they began to rejoice over their brethren, saying: Behold the time is past, and the words of Samuel are not fulfilled; therefore, your joy and your faith concerning this thing hath been vain. (3 Nephi 1:5–6)

26: Now it came to pass that there was a day set apart by the unbelievers, that all those who believed in those traditions should be put to death except the sign should come to pass, which had been given by Samuel the prophet. Now it came to pass that when Nephi, the son of Nephi, saw this wickedness of his people, his heart was exceedingly sorrowful. (3 Nephi 1:9–10)

27: And it came to pass that he went out and bowed himself down upon the earth, and cried mightily to his God in behalf of his people, yea, those who were about to be destroyed because of their faith in the tradition of their fathers. And it came to pass that he cried mightily unto the Lord all that day; and behold, the voice of the Lord came unto him, saying: Lift up your head and be of good cheer; for behold, the time is at hand, and on this night shall the sign be given, and on the morrow come I into the world, to show unto the world that I will fulfil all that which I have caused to be spoken by the mouth of my holy prophets. (3 Nephi 1:11–13)

28: Behold I come unto my own, to fulfil all things which I have made known unto the children of men from the foundation of the world, and to do the will, both of the Father and of the Son—of the Father because of me, and of the Son because of my flesh. And behold, the time is at hand, and this night shall the sign be given. (3 Nephi 1:14)

29: And it came to pass that the words which came unto Nephi were fulfilled, according as they had been spoken; for behold, at the going down of the sun there was no darkness; and the people began to be astonished because there was no darkness when the night came. And there were many, who had not believed the words of the prophets, who fell to the earth and became as if they were dead, for they knew that the great plan of destruction which they had laid for those who believed in the words of the prophets had been frustrated; for the sign which had been given was already at hand. (3 Nephi 1:15–16)

30: And it came to pass that there was no darkness in all that night, but it was as light as though it was mid-day. And it came to pass that the sun did rise in the morning again, according to its proper order; and they knew that it was the day that the Lord should be born, because of the sign which had been given. And it had come to pass, yea, all things, every whit, according to the words of the prophets. (3 Nephi 1:19–20)

31: For unto us a child is born, unto us a son is given: and the government shall be upon his shoulder: and his name shall be called Wonderful, Counsellor, The mighty God, The everlasting Father, The Prince of Peace. (Isaiah 9:6)

About the Author

Ashley Nicoll, Sunshine & Shade Photography

Rebecca Irvine lives in Mesa, Arizona, with her husband and three children. She is a graduate of Brigham Young University and served as a missionary for The Church of Jesus Christ of Latter-day Saints in the England London South Mission. Currently, Rebecca serves as the Primary president in her home ward. In addition to reading and writing, her hobbies include drawing, blogging, and working part-time as a market research analyst. *Family Home Evening Adventures* is Rebecca Irvine's second book.